THE SMART SHOPPER'S GUIDE TO THE BEST BUYS FOR KIDS

by Sue Robinson

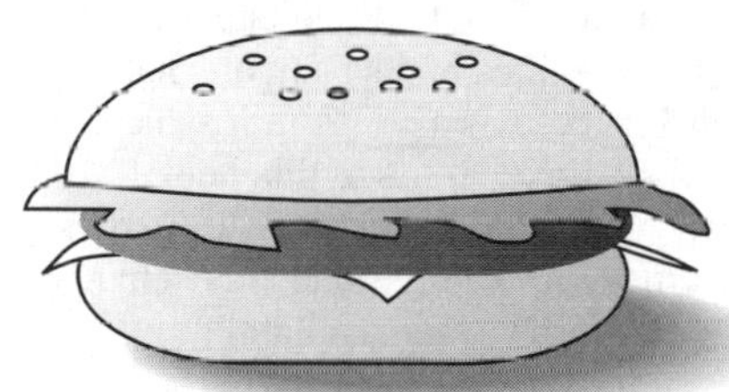

Macmillan/Spectrum

International Standard Book Number: 0-02-861287-6

Library of Congress Cataloging Card Number: 96-070006

98 97 96 9 8 7 6 5 4 3 2 1

Interpretation of the printing code: the rightmost number of the first series of numbers is the year of the book's printing; the rightmost number of the second series of numbers is the number of the book's printing. For example, a printing code of 96-1 shows that the first printing occurred in 1996.

Printed in the United States of America

Design by Amy Peppler Adams—designLab, Seattle

CONTENTS

This book is dedicated to the memory of:
Evelyn Goldman
1928-1996

A renaissance woman who sparked my interest in investigative reporting and taught me the fundamentals of in-depth research and organization.

ACKNOWLEDGMENTS

A great big thank-you to my beautiful and patient daughter, Marissa (the best kid who deserves the best buys), and my wonderful husband, Felix, who didn't see a home-cooked meal on the table during the writing of this book. I love you both and don't think about throwing away those take-out menus just yet. Thanks also to my parents, Marion and Arnold Friedman, who taught me how to seek out quality at the lowest possible prices; my sister Lori Frank, her husband George and their two precocious and witty children, Emily and Jason; Dorothy Evins, my lifelong friend who kept me laughing through the rough times, and her son Alex who helped me with the boy's point of view; Sandra Skydell whose love, support, encouragement and Friday night meals got me through this project; Buddy Skydell, who looked at the initial proposal for this book and said, "start banging this out, someone's going to buy it"; Mathew and Louise Evins of Evins Communication for their expert marketing advice and assistance; Dr. Steven Field, who assured me it was nothing; Dan Feinstein of *Newsday* for continuing support; Dan Hochsburg of Children's Emporium for showing me the ropes of off-price childrenswear; Ritz Carlton Hotels for showing me that kids and five-star hotels really can mix; Mona's Kids for cover fashion; Geiger for the exquisite, boiled wool cardigans seen on the back cover; Lillian Cohen, whose impeccable taste and attention to detail have inspired me since I was a child; Faith, Tom and Meredith Barnidge, the L.A. Connection; Chris Barranca of New York City's Kids Are Magic and my old friend, Andy Kaufman, whose untimely death robbed the world of a comic genius but motivated my decision to get on with life and have a child. To my editor, Debby Englander, whose foresight and belief in my work were integral in making this book a reality, I will always be grateful.

INTRODUCTION

The Best Things in Life Are Free—or Deeply Discounted

Congratulations, smart shopper! You have just picked up a guide that the world of retail doesn't want you to know about. *The Smart Shopper's Guide to the Best Buys for Kids* is an at-home reference tool for year-round family bargain shopping. You're about to learn about insider-only shopping information, strategies and listings of sample sales, warehouse events, factory store backrooms, off-price dealers, fine furniture discount opportunities, discounted mail/phone order merchants, hotel and airline specials, upscale catalog clearance centers, camp scholarships, toy bargains and lots more. By using this "insider" knowledge, you'll be able to save as much as 90% off regular retail prices!

Who doesn't want the best of everything for their children? I delivered my daughter around the same time that Christie Brinkley had her Alexa and Princess Diana gave birth to Prince Harry. "How will their lifestyles differ from my child's?" I wondered. Apart from the obvious celebrity status, what will these famous kids have that my child, and perhaps yours, won't?

While conspicuous consumption may not be a noble goal in life, don't our kids deserve the best life has to offer, too? You bet! This book is dedicated to all parents, grandparents, guardians and friends who want the best in designer fashion, first-class vacations, fine furnishings, gourmet foods and restaurants, toys, current hairstyles and summer camps without busting their budgets.

What makes me such an expert? Believe it or not, my bargain-hunting career actually began when I was a publicist for the Virgin/Atlantic record company in New York City. As a publicist, it was my job to generate as many print and broadcast reviews, interviews and mentions in the media as possible for the express purpose of selling our bands and their records, videos, CDs, etc. While escorting band members to and from various television studios and radio stations, I always had to make a wardrobe stop at the latest and hippest rock 'n' roll outfitter to get stage clothes for the members. "Hey, I can't go on Saturday Night Live looking like this!" they cried. If you think you've seen mind-boggling prices at upscale department stores, you should see what goes on at these "rip off the dumb young rock star emporiums!"

Being a genetically predisposed bargain-seeker, I simply could not keep my mouth shut while my rock 'n' roll clients were constantly being overcharged! While one band member was contemplating whether to buy a pink, fringed deerskin leather jacket, I quickly went into action. Since the store was empty, I assumed the manager wanted some business. I politely approached the manager and inquired, "What can you do about this price?" Faster than you can say "Cheap Trick," the manager took $50 off the price. Good, but not good enough, I thought. I continued this little song and dance until a full 40% came off the jacket price. Thus, my second career began.

From the wild world of rock 'n' roll, I entered the wonderful world of magazines. While at *Family Circle,* I learned that a little research can turn up the most incredible and useful information. When I had my daughter, Marissa, I decided to put these research skills to work uncovering children's bargains. All I needed was a way to deliver my discount secrets to other parents looking for great deals. And so I conceived and delivered my next baby, a pink and blue newsletter called, *Kid News—A Children's Bargain Guide.*

Not only did parents and grandparents clamor for my listings in the newsletter, but so did the media! *New York Newsday*'s, bargain-hunter columnist Dan Feinstein called it, "A gold mine of information." The newsletter took off, and I began making personal appearances on NBC's *Weekend Today, Eyewitness News, Good Morning America* (Weekend), *Fox Five News, NY 1 News,*

Lifetime television, and more! Shortly thereafter, I began writing children's consumer articles for other publications, including *Ladies Home Journal* and the *New York Daily News*. I even had my own radio spot during a segment called "Small Things Considered."

Essentially, I've been doing nothing but uncovering bargains across the country for the past eleven years! The fruits of my work are collected in this handy volume. To get the most out of *The Smart Shopper's Guide*, I strongly recommend that you consult the book whenever you're making travel plans, whether they're for vacation or business. If you're headed to a major metropolitan area, look in the index under apparel marts and sample sales and follow the directions on how to get into the showrooms in the trade buildings for savings up to 80% off on top designer kids clothes! Or look in the index for the region of the country you're visiting. Allow time to stop at your favorite toy company factory store, designer warehouse sale, furniture outlet etc. My sister Lori and I have been making yearly pilgrimages with our families to Lancaster, Pennsylvania each summer for a great low-cost family getaway and a visit to our favorite discount haunts to stock up on better-made kid clothes (Florence Eiseman, So Fun!, Flapdoodles, Hartstrings, Kitestrings, etc.) and furnishings for the upcoming school year. (See Lancaster, Pennsylvania in the Index for details.)

Even if you're stuck at home, this book will give you plenty of information. You can order directly over the phone from your favorite manufacturer or factory store and get discounts ranging from 40% to 80% off retail prices. If you're unfamiliar with the particular lines, most salespeople are adept at describing outfits down to the tiniest detail. They'll even give you precise washing and care instructions.

Planning a vacation? Don't make your reservation until you've checked with the hotel and airline consolidators in Chapter 3, "First-Class Kiddies." Then contact the local Convention and Visitor's bureaus or the coupon companies listed in this chapter for coupon books and vacation guides. Skim the tips and strategies for securing first-class hotel accommodations at value prices. I'm not kidding! Read through the recommendations and you'll see how you and your family can be treated like royalty when you stay at luxury hotels while still paying affordable rates.

If you want to furnish a nursery or redecorate your kid's room, but can't afford to hire a professional designer, read Chapter 2, "Suite Dreams." This chapter explains how most off-price dealers will send you catalogs or photostats of the children's furniture groups you're interested in. Make your selection, and the dealer will ship the furniture to your home at 40% to 50% savings. Did you know that many carpet and window treatment companies will send you samples to keep? Take them to your local retailers, compare prices and you'll be as shocked as I was to find that the same Levelor or Hunter Douglas blinds and shades are available at 50% to 80% off retail price!

To maximize the savings strategies in this book, I urge you to compile a universal gift list covering all friends and relatives. Keep the list in your wallet and pull it out whenever you go to any of the places listed in this guide. I keep one section of my closet to store clothes and toys picked up at sample sales, warehouse clearances, company toy outlets and catalog clearance stores. When my child is invited to a birthday party, we're always ready. And, you can bet that these items cost me at least half of what I would have paid to buy them at retail.

Also, you should be aware that no ad fees or any other monetary compensation were accepted in exchange for a listing in this book. As a consumer reporter, I would lose all credibility within the publishing industry if I were to accept payments for inclusion within this guide. It is my job to tell you the good, the bad and, at times, the ugly truth about discount shopping and bargains in general.

Businesses are constantly in flux. Prices change over time and stores fold and go under. I have made every effort to be up-to-date and accurate but, inevitably, some errors will occur. If you find an inaccuracy, please let us know so that we can make corrections in the next edition of this book. And if we've omitted a favorite bargain find of yours, let us know by writing to: KID NEWS, P.O. Box 797, Forest Hills, NY, 11375. We'll include your discovery in the next edition of *The Smart Shopper's Guide*.

See you at the bargain racks!
Sue Robinson

CHAPTER ONE

FIVE-STAR FASHION

There is a miracle *off* 34th Street that even Kris Kringle himself didn't know about. Gather round . . . here's the scoop: You can now buy upscale, designer and better-made fashion for children at 40% to 85% below regular retail department store prices. The secret is shopping at factory back rooms, warehouse clearances, off-price merchants, showroom sample and stock sales, on-site factory stores, retail closeout stores, apparel marts, off-site outlets and via discount mail and phone order opportunities all over the country.

My first experience with "true" discount shopping came at the age of three on Havermeyer Street in the Williamsburg section of Brooklyn, New York. If Bette Davis had walked in to this off-price children's outlet, she would have blurted out, "What a dump!" Throngs of fashionably attired mothers picking through piles of "uptown" designer children's clothes, crying babies, children trying on clothes in the aisles, husbands losing their tempers and a deserted alleyway that connected the girls' store to the boys' store behind impossibly heavy fire doors, were the hallmark of Natan Borlam's.

Cheap is small and not too steep
But best of all cheap is cheap
Circumstance has forced my hand
To be a cut price person in a low budget land
Times are hard and we'll all survive
I just got to learn to economize

—Ray Davies, The Kinks, "Low Budget"—Arista Records, 1979

Run on a tight budget, Borlam by necessity had rock-bottom overhead. Computerization was rejected in favor of hand-scribbled phone numbers of vendors, manufacturers and other business contacts on the wall next to the telephone. My parents used to joke that if Borlam's ever got a paint job they'd surely go out of business.

But my biggest complaint was the lack of dressing rooms. I had a lot to learn. If you want fancy service and amenities, you go to Saks Fifth Avenue and pay for it. If you want great bargains, you go where the rents are low and the savings are passed on to the consumer.

Fast-forward to 1985. I am shopping for a layette so that my newborn can leave New York University hospital in style come early Spring. The stretchies are adorable, the bedding is precious and the prices are outrageous! How can such tiny garments have such hefty hangtags? There has to be a less expensive way. As an experienced writer for a leading woman's magazine, I decided to put my research skills to the test and uncover the secrets behind buying childrenswear at affordable, if not downright cheap prices.

My research led me to my first back-room factory store in Long Island City. The lady at the reception desk looked at me skeptically as I cautiously requested permission to enter the back-room store. She warned me to be careful on my way back. Wending my way through the sewing machines and forklifts, I found myself learning more about childrenswear production than I anticipated. Bolts of fabric here, cutting patterns there and illegal aliens everywhere! At the end of my journey through the endless maze of garment racks and heavy machinery came the great reward. The same items I had recently seen at a pricey boutique for $65.00 were right in front of me for—are you ready—$5.00. Although it all felt faintly criminal, there was nothing unethical going on here at all. A manufacturer simply overproduced. To recoup the cost, the company was selling off these overruns and discarded samples.

As I continued my research, I found that dozens of other companies operated the same way. At this point, I knew that other parents would want to shop at these places too. I decided to start reporting these exciting finds to other economically stressed parents. My goal was to find the best of the best for kids at deeply discounted prices. Ladies and gentlemen, I present to you the greatest bargains (and a little shopping advice) to help you bring down the cost of dressing up your child.

Defensive Shopping Strategies and Tips to Save Big

All right, you're ready for the names and addresses of these great bargains . . . relax, your patience will be rewarded. Before you get to the listings, you've got to learn what it takes to be a smart shopper. Here's a rundown of the basics that you'll need to know before you hit those racks:

- Do your shopping homework. In order to assess how good a deal you're getting when using the resources in this book, it's essential that you visit local department stores and retail boutiques to familiarize yourself with pricing. Then, you can accurately comparison-shop. You should know the childrenswear designer names, labels and styles that you find appealing. (A good way to begin is by ordering the Children's Wear Digest catalog that features clear pictures with retail prices and manufacturer names of good brands mentioned throughout this book. Call 800-242-5437.) It's a good idea to carry a pen and pad to take notes. As you will see later, you can order discounted merchandise by phone or mail if you can describe what you want. (This won't be necessary when ordering discounted goods through catalogs.)
- Be skeptical of a children's retail store in a mall or other high-rent district claiming everyday discounts of 20%. Keep in mind that these stores couldn't make their overhead if they were giving out real bargains. Here's how many of these stores work. An item comes in for pricing. Instead of calculating the hangtag price by traditional doubling (keystoning) of the wholesale price, the store overinflates the numbers just enough so that by the time you take off that 20% reduction, you're actually paying the full retail price! What a scam!

- If you live in a city with a downtown merchandise, apparel mart or fashion center, call and inquire about sample sale policies. Some apparel marts hold biannual or quarterly group vendor sample sales. Get yourself on the mailing list for these. If possible, go directly to the "marts" and pick up a buyer's guide, which lists the manufacturers represented in the building. (You can also call for the directory; however some fashion marts may charge a nominal fee anywhere between $3.00 and $5.00.) Now pull out your notes and look up your favorite children's manufacturers in the index of the directory. Call and politely ask when the next sample sale will be held. The response will be either

  1. "You can come in now and browse through our samples."
  2. "We're planning one on . . . "
  3. "We don't do sample sales."

  As far as response #3 goes, don't get discouraged. The manufacturer may change its mind in the future, depending on returned goods, or, the person you spoke to may not have had the correct information. Hint: Try again.

  Remember that these trade buildings are not open to the public at large. It may be necessary to make an appointment in advance to visit a showroom. You may even have to get a pass issued by the salesperson. Dress nicely, behave in a business-like manner and you shouldn't have any problems. Absolutely no children are allowed in these showrooms.

- Do not be intimidated by price tags in retail establishments!

  You should be outraged, perplexed or dismayed, but never intimidated at a retail establishment. Ask yourself, "Does this price sound right? Can I do better somewhere else?" The answer most of the time should be a resounding yes! Ask the retail store owner if he will come down on the sticker price. Explain that you love the outfit but it is somewhat beyond your budget. Don't expect a major markdown here.

Generally 20% off is the most you can count on as a reduction; just try and get the tax thrown in as an added incentive for you to buy. Hint: This strategy works best at off-hours or when the store is fairly empty—when the sales people are more motivated to make a sale. In larger department stores or chains like the Gap, find out when the merchandise will be reduced for sale. In my neighborhood the sales girls tell me that inventory is marked down every Tuesday evening after the store closes. I make sure to get there early on Wednesday if there's something in particular I want.

- If haggling doesn't work, don't despair. Call the manufacturer on the garment hangtag and ask if it has an outlet store. If so, call the store closest to you and ask if they have the outfit you want and whether it can be shipped to you at the reduced outlet price.
- Create a universal gift list for friends and family and stockpile fabulous bargain finds throughout the year. Many of the warehouse sales, sample sales and other resources in this book will have additional surprises in store for you. For example, The Tickle Me! Tackle Me! warehouse clearance sales not only sell off the children's collections at deep discounts, but practically give away coordinating accessories such as hairbows, barrettes, belts, socks, footwear, sunglasses, costume jewelry, hats, visors and more. You should plan ahead and buy in bulk for upcoming birthday gifts, stocking stuffers, party favors, baby gifts, holiday presents, you name it! Simply box them away and pull out when you need the gifts.
- Buy with an eye toward the future. If you come across a sensational bargain, consider purchasing larger sizes to accommodate your child's unavoidable growth spurts. You'll save yourself money and time, especially when Junior parades out of his room in pants that are two inches too short (when did he grow?) and you remember that great bargain you had the foresight to bring home in a bigger size!

- Don't turn your nose up at seconds, irregulars or even damaged goods. Minor imperfections that qualify garments to be relinquished to the seconds or irregular racks are often imperceptible to the average consumer. A misplaced backstitch, yarn from a different dye lot or a washable smudge can help bring an already reduced price down even further. If something is really damaged, you've just got to be creative. Go to your local trim and fabric store to find dozens of ways to repair holes attractively and easily. Iron-on appliqués, patches and whimsical buttons can fix a hole and enhance the garment's design at the same time. These items also make ideal play clothes, gym uniforms (who cares about a pair of sweat pants with a tiny hole?), and general camp and home knock-about duds.

- Ask to be placed on mailing lists at any retail and wholesale venues you visit. Many places offer birthday club discounts, frequent buyer programs, reminder notices with accompanying discount coupons, and special event and advance sale notices for mailing list customers only.

  Dan Hochsberg, owner and manager of Brooklyn's premier off-price kid's clothing store, Children's Emporium, explains, "We send out notices after buying trips and to announce our two annual blow-out sales. It's important to come in immediately after receiving these notices for best selection." We will remind you throughout this guide which manufacturers have mailing lists. It's a good idea to get on these lists immediately after reading about each company that intrigues you.

- Don't disregard larger retailers such as Mervyn's, JC Penney, Wal-Mart, Target, Sears, Kids 'Я' Us and their accompanying private label lines. Many private labels are bought directly from the same factory in Malaysia, let's say, that produces the more upscale, famous name collections seen in pricey chain and department stores. By going directly to the factory and eliminating the middlemen, these mass merchants can offer you high-quality garments at significant savings!

- Flea markets are a great place to find first-quality children's clothes, accessories and shoes at discount prices. In fact, many children's designers and manufacturers end up there when the economy is sluggish. Some off-price stores such as Mona's Kids of East Meadow, New York, Boca Raton and Coral Springs, Florida actually got their start at flea markets. They brought in salesmen's samples from the finest children's lines and sold them at 50% off retail. So pay close attention at your next flea market excursion.

- Networking with other parents at sales events is a must. After all, they may know something that you don't. To break the ice you could offer a bargain pearl of information and they may be inclined to do the same. Don't be shy; you and your bank account have a lot to gain. Hint: I find this to be easiest to do while waiting in line to pay for my purchases.

- Always bring along items from your childrens' closet for comparison sizing when you can't bring your children to the factory or warehouse. This way you'll be assured of a reasonably good fit.

- Save those children's fashion catalogs. As you are about to find out, many upscale children's collections such as Oilily, Geiger, Wooden Soldier, Patagonia, Strasburg Lace and Storybook Heirlooms have outlets, overstocks departments or manufacturer warehouse sales where you can buy merchandise from past seasons (sometimes the current one as well) at discounted prices. Just browse through the catalogs, decide what you like and visit the sale location or order directly by phone.

- Read! Read! Read! When I travel, the first thing I do after hotel registration is grab the local and regional newspapers, magazines and brochures. Scanning these periodicals for local warehouse events and sales has become a passion as well as an integral part of my bargain-hunting business. Make it a part of your business and you might come across something I've missed. Let me know and we'll publish your findings in the next edition of this book.

All Good Things Must Come to an End (a.k.a. Deathwatch of a Ridiculously Overpriced Children's Store)

Here's a way to really clean up on the highest quality kid duds at rock-bottom prices. From the moment a store opens its doors, a good shopper can figure out whether the store is going to fly, or crash, in the neighborhood. If the store is in your neighborhood, you probably know the shopping habits of your fellow consumers. Are they likely to part with hundreds of dollars to wardrobe their kids? Maybe they are in Beverly Hills, Palm Beach or Madison Avenue, but certainly not in my neighborhood and probably not in yours either.

Next, determine whether the store is occupying prime real estate territory and look at the amount of square footage. A store needs to sell a lot of expensive clothes to support the overhead and make a profit. There was a textbook example of this situation in my neighborhood a few years back. An exquisitely outfitted children's store opened in a 2,000-square-foot space on a bustling and expensive rental avenue. Folks went in to browse, ooh and ah, but no one bought. My countdown began. I started to make mental notes of items I would purchase once the death knell sounded. Sure enough, less than a year later, the markdowns began. Toward the end, the owners became so desperate that they simply walked up to customers (myself included) and pleaded, "Make me an offer." Who could refuse?

Outlet Caveat

Appearances May Be Deceiving

Even in an outlet store, don't assume that everything's a great deal. Here's where it pays to do your shopping homework and learn about various fabric grades, qualities and differences. One outfit in an outlet store may be strikingly similar to what appears to be the same outfit in a retail store. However, the two may not be identical. Start by checking labels for fabric content. Designers admit that they make different goods for the outlet stores. I don't think you're getting a real bargain with these "made for outlet" items. You're getting exactly what you pay for now, a garment that looks like the one you saw uptown, but made from an inferior fabric.

You Better Shop Around!

I remember browsing through a Calvin Klein outlet store scrutinizing hangtags and wondering, "Where are the bargains?" Prices seemed inordinately high for a so-called discount store. Much to my surprise, I've found that some garments cost more at some outlet stores than at retail department stores (where sales can reduce items to very competitive prices). Once again, never assume you're automatically getting a price break because you're in an outlet store or outlet mall. Familiarize yourself with retail prices as well as department store sale prices to make sure you're getting a real deal.

Oldies Are Not Goodies in the Discount Game

Is a discounted item a bargain if it has been lying around the outlet for several seasons or even years? No matter how classic a style may be, if it's old, it's probably shopworn and not worth the investment. Watch out for this. Outlets have a habit of selling goods from past seasons that some historic preservation groups would love to get their hands on. Let them.

Breaking the Dress Code: Terms to Know Before You Go . . . Bargain Hunting, That Is

To assist you in your quest for the great American bargain, you need to understand the key "insider fashion terminology" so that you'll understand the type of merchandise offered at the various sales listed in this book. With this information, you'll be able to distinguish "good deals" from the "duds." Most of you have never attended a real sample sale (a good deal), but have shopped those 20% off every day discount stores (duds). The following is a brief and revealing education in basic, contemporary retail merchandising and price structuring to help you become a smart shopper who will never pay retail prices again!

- **Retail.** This is the price at which stores offer merchandise for sale to the consumer. The retail price is generally arrived at by doubling the wholesale price. (This is also known as *keystoning.*)

- **Wholesale.** Wholesale refers to the sale of goods in large quantities directly to retailers and jobbers, not consumers. The manufacturer figures the profit margin needed and adds it on to the cost of making the goods to arrive at the wholesale price. Most retailers then double the wholesale price to calculate the consumer price. However, as you will see, some retailers inflate this wholesale number further.

- **Below Wholesale** (BW). This is just what it sounds like. Many outlets, sample sales and off-price merchants mentioned in this book will be selling items at wholesale prices, approximately 50% off retail prices, or below wholesale. This means anything from under wholesale prices; greater than 50% off; cost prices (what it actually cost the manufacturer to make the item without a profit) or even below cost, up to 90% off retail, when merchandise is being cleared out and the manufacturer or merchant wants to recoup whatever cash he can.

- **Samples.** "Samples" describes garments that are made for sales people to show and sell to retail store buyers. Sometimes, samples never make it into the actual clothing line if, for example, the garment was too expensive or difficult to produce. One of the perks of shopping sample sales is that you can purchase samples that were never mass-produced at incredibly low prices and walk away with a one-of-a kind garment.
- **Clearance Rack.** Clearance racks hold leftover goods from the previous selling season that are sold at 50% to 85% off original retail prices. Prices are usually so low that you should buy extra items as gifts for your child to grow into.
- **Closeouts, Discontinued or Special Purchase.** There are stores, (often off-price merchants and discounters), that purchase specific items from a manufacturer at a very low cost for the exclusive purpose of putting them on sale. These may be discontinued items that the manufacturer does not plan to carry forward the following season, irregulars, or first-quality leftovers. (These "loss-leaders" also help lure customers into the store.)
- **Irregulars.** Irregular merchandise may not have passed inspection based on the manufacturer's rigid standards. Some flaws can be as minor and invisible to the average consumer as a backstitch or a spot that can be easily removed. I've seen perfect merchandise at warehouse sales marked as irregular because the sizing on the label was incorrect. This big-deal problem to the manufacturer translates into big-deal savings for you. Prices on irregulars can go as low as 90% off retail. So don't overlook irregular merchandise or you might miss some great buys.
- **Damaged.** Damaged goods are items with visible imperfections. Stores sell these at drastic reductions. If you're creative, or skilled with a needle, consider bringing these bargains home for a quick fix-up.

- **Overruns, Leftovers, Overages.** These are manufacturer overcuts that haven't been sold by the end of the season. Many off-price merchants and outlets take these overruns off the manufacturer's hands at very reduced rates, often way below wholesale. (Not surprisingly, the retail department stores get angry because they bought the same merchandise at a higher price at the beginning of the selling season.) Although there may only be a six- to eight-week difference in shipping schedules, the same merchandise may be found at both retail and off-price stores at dramatically different price points. You can expect to pay around 40% to 50% off retail prices on these first-quality overruns.

- **Past Season or Out of Season.** A past-season item for an outlet store is usually in season for most consumers. Many retail stores purchase merchandise a full season ahead. You've all seen winter coats in stores during the heat waves of August. By the time early Fall rolls around, these clothes are considered to be out of season. The off-price merchants and outlet store buyers take this merchandise off the manufacturer's hands. I don't know about you, but I have a much keener interest in purchasing winter clothes when there's a nip in the air than when weather forecasters are still giving out sunburn indexes. You'll save big money by playing the waiting game.

- **Preview Sales.** Previews are early looks at next season's styles, promoted through special sales at the retail level. Don't expect huge markdowns at these sales. Do expect to find more than 20% to 30% off regular retail prices.

- **Markup Cancellation.** Markup cancellation is "a downward price adjustment that offsets an original inflated markup that is more normal," according to the textbook *Mathematics for Retail Buying*, Fourth Edition, by Bette K. Tepper & Newton E. Godnick (Fairchild Publications, New York, 1994). This is how discount stores operate. They overinflate the price of an item (more than double the wholesale price, for instance) and print that arbitrary figure on the hangtag as the regular retail price, from which you can now deduct their everyday 20% discount. Gee, thanks a lot!

- **You Do the Math.** If an item is bought from a manufacturer at $7 and the store claims the item's retail price is $22, and you can knock off 20% due to the magnanimous discount policy, then you'll pay $17.60. Well, guess what, if you double the wholesale price of $7 to a normal markup of $14, you're still not getting a discount! However, on the hangtag, this lowered price of $17.60 seems to be a great deal, to uneducated shoppers that is. Caveat emptor! Bargain hunter, beware!

Where the Buys Are

East Coast Region

Aida & Jimmy's Off-Price Specialty Store
41 West 28th Street
2nd Floor
New York City, NY 10001
(212) 689-2415

Hours: Mon.–Sat. 9–6
(Closed Sat. in July & Aug)
Payment: Major credit cards

A great resource for dresses in all styles and all sizes from infant through preteen and junior girls. Aida & Jimmy specialize in better-made dresses at 50% below manufacturer's list price starting at $15 and on up to $150. The store claims to have one of the largest selections of girl's dress wear in New York, and we agree. Some brand names offered include Dorissa, Nicole and Sylvia Whyte. There is a limited supply of Baby Togs boyswear from infant through size 7. If you mention this book, the store will deduct 10% off your total bill for a super bargain.

Amelia Warehouse Sale
Route 681
Amelia, VA 23002
(804) 561-5060

This nationally famous warehouse sale takes place three times a year, usually in November, March and August. Call the above number and place your name on the mailing list, then get ready to get in line early for unbelievable dress bargains. You'll find "Star" holiday, velvet and cotton frocks in the $9–$17 price range. All sizes available, from 12 months up through preteen. No out-of-state checks accepted, so bring cash.

Baby Steps Factory Store
45 Spruce Street
Ridgefield Park, NJ 07660
(201) 641-6991

Hours: Mon.–Fri. 10–2
Payment: Cash

These are the manufacturers of well-designed pajamas, nightgowns, infant layette, long underwear and durable playwear. High-style prints and rich colors distinguish Baby Steps from other playwear and pajama makers. All sizes are from newborn to 14. Figure on saving 30%–40% by going directly to this factory store. Watch your step climbing the staircase. Sometimes you have to work a little for your bargains. If you mention this book the store will deduct an additional 5% from your total purchase. Once again, no tax—you're in Jersey! Cash payments only.

Bebe Chic
Factory Backroom Store
115 River Road
Suite 1204
Edgewater, NJ 07020
(201) 941-5414

Hours: Mon.–Fri. 10–3:30
Payment: Checks, no credit cards

Outfit your baby's stroller in these elegant, quilted carriage covers at next-to-nothing prices. Bebe Chic also manufactures bedding, bumpers, diaper bags, fabrics, toweling, sheets, etc. They used to have a lot of inventory in the store; however, they tell us that supplies may be somewhat limited at times. You'd be wise to call first to make sure they have what you're looking for.

Benetton Outlet Store
40–06 Main Street
Flushing, NY 11354
(near Roosevelt Avenue)
(718) 461-7777

Payment: AmEx, MC, no checks

Most New Yorkers are under the impression that they have to travel to Vermont to realize big savings on the finest line of imported Italian children's wear around. But tucked away in Flushing, Queens is the real deal—a Benetton outlet store where you can purchase the otherwise very pricey Italian knit sweaters, wool kilts, jumpers, blazers, sweat suits and accessories at 50% off and more. You'll find current goods (the outlet receives shipments after all retail stores have been stocked), and past-season goods (when the clothes are this beautiful and well constructed, does it really matter?) There's a municipal parking lot nearby for your convenience. And don't forget to stop by Taipan's Bakery around the corner for the finest, and most colorful, in Asian baking (kids love this place). Their pastel-colored, checker-board sponge cake is so light it prac-tically floats off the shelf, and it's only $8! Another great bargain!

Bib 'N Tucker
Seasonal Warehouse Sales
Mailing List
123 Hudson Street
Hackensack, NJ 07601
(201) 941-0855

Payment: Major credit cards

Get yourself on the mailing list for announcements of Bib 'N Tucker's seasonal warehouse sales where you can pick up infant layette, bibs, robes, denim appliquéd outfits, assorted toddler wear and accessories at 50% off department store retail prices. Sales have traditionally taken place in the Spring and Fall.

Big Enough
Outlet Store
700 Canal Street
Stamford, CT 06902
(203) 353-0628 or
(800) 288-7321

Catalog phone orders accepted

Big Enough is cute enough but not cheap enough . . . until now. For drastic reductions on samples, seconds (minor imperfections—you probably won't notice) and overruns from the 100% cotton Big Enough collection, stop by the store. Or, familiarize yourself with the line through their catalog (start collecting—and keeping—catalogs by getting yourself placed on the regular mailing lists) and order at discounted prices right over the phone. A precise sizing system makes mail/phone orders foolproof. Styles, fabric and tailoring get high marks here. I especially love their waffle thermal dresses, tartan skate skirts, brushed twill kilts and jumpers. For boys, striped crew tops in sage and black, brushed twill trousers and reversible hooded sweatshirts are super. A summer winner for girls is the sleeveless tank with lace-up back (oh so Vera Wang!) Now for the best part: Current samples and seconds are half the regular retail price, and once they go out of season, prices plunge to half of that! If you're in the store, make sure to rummage through the bins for $2 treasures!

Black Parrot Discounter
328 Main Street
Rockland, ME 04841
(207) 594-9161

Hours: Mon.–Sat. 10–6
Payment: Visa, MC, checks
Phone orders accepted

If you love the creations of Black Parrot, then visit or call their store, where you can purchase past-season goods at up to 60% off retail. You can also pick up some exclusive Black Parrot items made specifically for the store and sold at low, low price points. If you're not familiar with the line, their designs feature beautiful outerwear such as reversible Polartec with corduroy, velvet, wool or supplex nylon shell, which functions as either a dressy or casual coat! This particular coat is versatile enough to take your kid from school to the opera. Other lines found at the store include: MN Bird (puckered bathing suits seen at upscale department stores), Zutano, Luli, Ruth Hornbein sweaters (exquisite works of art made from chenille, angora and cotton), Baby Armadillo and Bottom Buddies.

Branded Garments Orchard Motorcycle Backroom Factory Store
36–06 43rd Ave. (one block north of Queens Blvd.)
Long Island City, NY 11101
(718) 361-2072

Phone orders accepted.

For your little rebel with or without a cause, here's your chance to buy top of the line, deerskin-leather motorcycle and fringed western jackets along with leather vests, skirts and, something new, nylon flight (bomber) jackets in assorted colors at the lowest prices. I fell in love with a fringed pink leather jacket that I had seen elsewhere for more than twice the factory store price! Expect to pay half of what you would in boutiques and department stores. They carry sizes 2-14 and accept most charges. Out-of-towners can call and order by phone.

Bugle's Boutique
Off-Price Merchant
Cranberry Mall
Route 19—Freedom Road
Cranberry, PA 16060
(412) 772-9666

Hours: Open daily 10–9; Sun. 12–5
Payment: Visa, MC, Discover, AmEx, and checks

Parkway Center Mall
Kinney Road
Greentree, PA 15220
(412) 920-7589

Sound the trumpets for the incredible bargains you'll find at Bugle's. The energetic owner of this upscale boutique will travel anywhere for closeouts and overruns from better brands featured at high-ticket boutiques and seen in The Wooden Soldier and Storybook Heirlooms catalogs. Everything is pre-ticketed, so you'll see the amazing reductions (and sometimes the original retail source) right away. Expect to pay about 40% to 50% off suggested retail and catalog prices for such great lines as Rubbies, Three Blind Mice, Childhood Enchantment, Tickle Me!, Tackle Me!, Warm Heart, Hearts Design, Eagles Eye, Hollywood Babe, Flapdoodles, Weather Tamer, Northern Isles and more. Don't forget to have a look around their clearance room, which offers discounts of 75% off all year round.

Carinho Outlet Store
254 Smith Street (between Court & Degraw)
Brooklyn, NY
(718) 855-6862

Catalog phone and mail orders accepted

Looking for newborn, "take me home" outfits and beautiful infant layette items? Carinho sells infant through size 4 imported knitwear in 100% cotton and acrylic designs at wholesale and below wholesale prices. You'll find everything that can be knitted for babies here, including bubbles, rompers, sweater sets, christening gowns, boys' knit tuxedos, blankets and booties. You'll also find the ultimate five-piece, home-from-the-hospital ensemble consisting of a two-piece outfit, hat, shawl and outer shawl made of lace, embroidery, silk and 100% cotton. Prices here start at $18. Call for the free color catalog and they will ship your order UPS, ASAP.

Children's Emporium Off-Price Stores
291-293 Court Street (Cobble Hill)
Brooklyn, NY 11231
(718) 875-8508

Hours: Mon.–Fri. 10–6:30; Sat. 10:30–5:30; Sun. 12–4
Payment: Major credit cards and checks
Phone orders accepted

Children's Emporium can outfit your child from head to toe in the finest imports and American designer clothing at up to—are you ready?—85% off department store prices! If it's Winter wear you need, they always carry the cozy and fashionable Brambilla down coats at 40% off. If you can wait until the winter season is underway, they will deduct additional dollars to bring prices down around wholesale. This store has everything from sleepwear to school clothes to dress-up, and an assortment of styles to suit every taste. They are renowned for giving the deepest discounts on Flapdoodles, Chevignon, Lorilynn, Bella Bambina, Petite Boy, My Boy Sam, Galipette, Kidokay, Canoli, Eagles Eye, Basic Elements, Mollygoggles handknit sweaters (60% off!), Breaking Waves swimsuits, Baby Steps pajamas, C'est Chouette, Coco Le Chat, Country Kids socks and tights, Elsy coats and so on, ad infinitum. Their shoe store is right next door, where such illustrious brands as Elefanten, Guess, Jonathan B, Rachels (see the cover of this book for an example of their great-looking shoes), Keds, Baby Botte, Right Step, Shoe Be Doo, Padders, Sara's Prints slippers, Buckle My Shoe, Vennetini (you've got to see these boots!) and Zappers can be had at 50% off and lower! A Children's Emporium best bet is the Country Kids socks and tights at wholesale prices. You can call up and order by phone if you know what you want. Children's Emporium has layaway plans. Bring in this book and receive an extra 10% off your total purchase.

Children's Wear Digest—Company Store
1543 Parham Road
Richmond, VA 23229
Hours: Mon.–Fri. 10–8; Sat 10–6
(804) 282-6887
Catalog: (800) 242-5437

Payment: Visa, MC, checks

The buyers for the Children's Wear Digest catalog know exactly what makes kids look great, and the catalog offerings reflect their fine taste. A nice surprise for those of you wishing that price points were a bit lower is the discovery of a company store where current catalog merchandise is reduced by 25% in season and on up to 80% off toward the end of season. Be a smart shopper and scoop up the great bargains in larger sizes and sock em' away until needed—don't forget your universal gift list. If you can't get to the store, don't panic; order the catalog anyway and wait for the sales in the book where you can still stock up on larger sizes for future use and save upwards of 60% off original retail prices. You'll find collections from such great kid labels as Patsy Aiken, Hartstrings, Mulberribush, Viaggi, Frog Pond, Flapdoodles, EIEIO, Sweet Potatoes, S.P.U.D.Z, Florence Eiseman, Sahara Club, Speedo, Leggoons, Cary, Gottex, Backflips, Laura Dare, Tom & Jerry, Sara's Prints, Chicken Noodle, Yazoo—enough?

Chock Catalog Discount Store
74 Orchard Street
New York, NY 10002
(212) 473-1929
Mail order (800) 222-0020

You don't have to be in New York City to take advantage of these well-priced layette, hosiery, bedding, and underwear items for children of all sizes. Louis Chock has been selling quality undergarments since 1921. They're the experts that can tell you that all cottons are not created equally. (Do you know the difference between carded, pima and upland cottons? They do and they'll be happy to explain it all to you and how it affects your underwear.) These underwear mavens sell Carters, Tic Tac Toe, Gerber, Lollipop and Buster Brown at 25% off retail via mail or phone. They are happy to answer all of your questions on the confusing subject of layette and anything else regarding underwear and cotton. Call or write for their free catalog.

Cotton Tales-Zinnias Factory Store
161–11 29th Ave.
Flushing, NY 11358
(718) 746-8551

Hours: Mon–Fri. 8–4:30
Payment: Checks, cash, no credit cards

A.K.A. Zinnias, you've probably seen these stylish cotton leggings, tunics, tie-dyed sweats, fringed t-shirts, crocheted bathing cover-ups and velour separates in those oh-so-trendy children's boutiques at oh-so-trendy prices! Those boutique owners don't want you to know that you can get it all for a lot less at the company's factory store in Flushing, New York. Don't overlook the bins on the floor for extra-special savings! I especially love their unusual, colorful, tie-dyed scrunchies that match each outfit. They also do bathing suits for the summer, plus shorts and t-shirts priced just right for knocking around at camp or the playground.

Country Kids Outlet Stores
10 Main Street
New Paltz, NY

Hours: Mon.–Fri. 9–5
Payment: Checks

This high-fashion hosiery company has opened their first outlet store where they sell off their complete line at wholesale prices. If you appreciate well-constructed and "wear-like-iron" tights that hold up wash after wash, then Country Kids is for you. Also known for their innovative and wild designs, professional stylists often choose these tights for children's fashion layouts in trade and consumer magazines. Prices in the store start at $2 for tights and socks that regularly go for $6.95 in department stores and boutiques (this is a bit below wholesale). The store occasionally stocks other bargains like legging and turtleneck overages.

Designer Kids Direct Off-Price Merchant and Factory Outlet
147 Plymouth Avenue
Fall River, MA 02721
(508) 673-7890

Hours: Mon.–Sat 10–5; Sun. 12 – 5
Payment: Visa, MC, checks

Specializing in trendy, 100% cotton clothing for boys size 12 months–12 years, and girls size 12 months–18 years, this true factory outlet store discounts 50% off and more all year long. Now, if you've been doing your shopping homework, you should recognize some of the labels here such as EIEIO, Hot Tots, Lorilyn Collection (did I hear some oohs and ahs?), Miss Mad, Erin's Babies, Mistee-vus and more. Known for their spectacular blow-out sales (50% below wholesale), in December and June you'll also find racks with $5.00 and $10.00 specials. Phone orders may be possible.

Dorothy's Tots To Teens
5300 Sunrise Highway
Massapequa Park, NY 11762
(516) 541-6128

Hours: Sat., Mon. 10–6; Thurs.–Fri. 10–9; Sun. 11–6
Payment: Major credit cards

Realize savings from 25% to 50% off throughout the year on such brands as Boss by I.G. Design, Smith, Stevenson, Tag Rag, Monkeywear, Tailfeathers, Gasoline and Once Upon A Kid. This one's a favorite of the preteen set, although they have plenty of discounted goods for the little tikes as well.

Down East Factory Outlet
916 North Ninth Street
Reading, PA 19604
(610) 372-1144

Hours: Mon.–Sat 9:30–5:30; Sun. 9:30–noon
Payment: Visa, MC, Discover
Phone orders accepted

While your Olympic hopeful goes for the gold, you can save your gold by shopping at this outlet, which specializes in professional gymnastics and skating gear for performance, competition and everyday workouts. If you're familiar with GK Elite Sportswear, you know that they design the best-fitting and most attractive activewear for the serious student and competitor. Many of my subscribers have been begging for information on this one, and now that my daughter is competing, I understand why—this stuff does not come cheap. Here's what we found: a sleeveless, crushed velvet leotard with scooped back was $23 at retail; Down East had it for $10! Matching headwear is also available—buy three scrunchies for $6, while at retail they go for $3 apiece. Call 800-345-4087 and order the GK Elite sportswear catalog (you may want to specify gymnastic or skating preference) for reference purposes, then call the outlet store directly where they sell samples, irregulars and first-quality merchandise at 35%–70% off suggested retail prices! Down East also carries a line of ski wear (an avalanche of savings), sneakers and shoes.

Eastern Apparel Company Wholesale Warehouse Sales
70 Highway 10
Whippany, NJ 07981
(201) 386-1000

Payment: Visa and MC
Hours: Get on mailing list to receive postcards with dates and hours of sale

This true wholesale warehouse opens its doors to an anxious public anywhere from six to eight times a year. The owners tell us that you can pretty much count on the sales taking place in February, March, April, May, August, September, October and November. You'll need to call and put your name on their mailing list for advance notification. They promise savings of 50%–70% on numerous better brands fed from their retail division (which they requested we not mention). However, all this translates to good news and big savings for you. Expect to see such stylish lines as Wes & Willy, Monkeywear, Baby Steps,

Brambilla, JM Originals, Flapdoodles and on and on.

Euro Bebe
Off-Price Store
53 Liberty Village
Flemington, NJ 08822
(908) 806-4688

Hours: Mon.–Sun. 10–6
Payment: Visa, MC, checks

Your baby can be a "Euro Bebe" at very American savings of 40% to 50% off retail prices at this tres chic boutique! Petite Bateau and other upscale imports such as Pomme Framboise and Petit Faune (how much do you love this line?) are here in sizes ranging from one month up to 14 years. You may want to factor in additional savings here because you're in Jersey—there's no sales tax collected! Make sure to put your name on their mailing list for advance sale notices and additional deductions.

Flapdoodles
Factory Stores
Rockvale Square
35 South Willowdale
Lancaster, PA 17602
(717) 390-7073

Hours: Mon.–Sat. 9:30–9;
Sun. 12–5
Payment: Visa, MC, Discover, AmEx, checks

International Designers Outlet
5211 International Drive
C-1-2
Orlando, FL 32819
(407) 352-0957

Hours: Mon.–Sat, 10–9;
Sun. 11–6
Payment: Visa, MC, Discover, AmEx, checks

Silver Sands Factory Outlets
10562 West Emerald Coast Parkway
Suite 119
Destin, FL 32541
(904) 837-5369

Hours: Mon.–Sat. 10–9;
Sun 10–6
Payment: Visa, MC, Discover, AmEx, checks

This 100%-cotton line has gone through multiple design changes through the years, and they finally seem to be getting it right. Having started out as a basic legging and turtleneck line, they have expanded their fashion scope to accommodate parents and kids with more sophisticated tastes. They now manufacture everything from swimsuits to outerwear, and you can purchase this popular line at the outlet stores for 30% to 50% off department store prices. They carry past-season and current goods in sizes infant to 16.

Flapdoodles Warehouse
Delaware Industrial Park
Call for exact directions
(302) 737-8125

Payment: Visa, MC and personal checks for a minimum purchase of $50

Some parents flip for Flapdoodles! If you're a fan of this 100% cotton sportswear line for boys and girls, then you may want to make a trip to the warehouse event that occurs approximately once a month, usually on the weekend. You'll need to call the above number, which will give you the exact dates for upcoming sales, as well as directions. Be forewarned, there are no public rest rooms, only great savings—wholesale and below.

Florence Eiseman
Factory Store
Tanger Factory Stores
312 Outlet Drive
Lancaster, PA 17602
(717) 295-9809

Phone/mail orders accepted.

Florence Eiseman belongs in the childrenswear Hall of Fame (if there were one). Her famous floral appliqué dresses and swimsuits have been worn by society and celebrity kids forever. Now your kids can have them at 30% to 40% below better department store prices with just a phone call. The very helpful staff at the Pennsylvania store (they have only two outlets—this one and a store in Indiana) will tell you what they've got, charge you $5 for a box and squeeze in as many discounted goodies as they can fit! Wait until the end of the season and realize discounts as high as 50% off retail. Eiseman has started designing coats that are equally as magnificent as her dresses. Sizes for girls start at infant and go up to size 14; boys, however, go up to only size 7. This is first-quality merchandise, although they are a year behind. Note: Florence Eiseman styles are classic; it matters not whether you purchase current or three years behind, her designs withstand the test of time—beautifully. After all, a classic by any other name (such as a "past-season item") is still a classic.

Gabriel Brothers Off-Price Chains
(unlisted phone numbers)
Winchester, VA
Weirtown, WV
Morgantown, WV
Clarksburg, WV
Fairmont, WV
Parkersburg, WV
Cumberland, MD
Kent, OH
St. Claresville, OH
Uniontown, PA
W. Miflin, PA
Belle Vernon, PA
Washington, PA
Philadelphia, PA
Harrisburg, PA

Ready for a magical mystery tour to the greatest savings for you and the kids? Step right this way! Talk about insider trading information. This chain of seriously off-price children's merchandise is quite controversial. Gabriel's is a chain of off-price stores selling top-brand kid clothes at deep discounts. In fact, they don't even publish their phone numbers. The owners explain that the stores are in such small towns that all you need to do is stop anyone on the street and ask, "Which way to Gabriel's!" We suggest a local gas station. I tested this by calling a local information operator and sure enough, she knew all about the place. It seems that they discount high-style kid clothes at up to 70% every day of the year. Let us know your evaluation of the stores and we'll print your response in the next edition.

Geiger Overstocks Department
Pond Lane
Middlebury, VT 06753
(802) 388-3156 (ask for the overstocks department)

Hours: Mon.–Sat. 10–5
Mail and phone orders accepted

Geiger of Austria manufactures exquisite boiled wool outerwear, jackets and cardigans with fanciful print and appliqué design finished with braided trim and pewter or novelty buttons. Each is a work of art and you can buy past-season styles at 50% off or more. These classic silhouettes are timeless and only you will know that they're last season's. Call for a color catalog; if they're out, they'll be happy to send you black and white workbooks instead.

Hanna Andersson Outlet
Artisan Outlet Village
72 Mirona Rd.
Portsmouth, NH 03801
(603) 433-6642

One hour outside of Boston, you'll find huge savings from this well-known Swedish designer of 100% cotton kids' wear at 20%–50% off catalog prices. Hanna Andersson consistently wins high praise from parents for the expert tailoring of their layette, outerwear, leggings, skirts, dresses, pants, hosiery, you name it! (If you have an infant, you must try their baby pilot caps in soda-fountain pastels or colorful primaries.) The store also participates in the Hannadowns program. Simply bring in your used Hannas and you'll receive a 20% credit toward your next retail or catalog purchase. Also, if your transaction takes place at the store, shipping is free of charge anywhere in the United States (This does not apply to sale merchandise, however—the clipped or black-marked tickets.)

Hartstrings/Baby Hartstrings/Kitestrings Factory Outlets
35 S. Willowdale Avenue
Rockvale Center
Lancaster, PA 17602
(717) 394-3366

821 Lancaster Avenue
Stratford, PA 19087
(610) 971-9400

832 Oley Street
Bldg. #4—2nd floor
Reading, PA 19064
(610) 376-8808

8 Dexter Lane
Kittery, ME 03904
(207) 439-0600

4565 Highway 1
Rehoboth Beach, DE 19971
(302) 644-0666

Niagara International Factory Outlets
1990 Military Road
Niagara Falls, NY 14304
(716) 297-0900

You gotta have Hart . . . strings! If you love refined, classic, coordinated sportswear looks, then be sure to put these true factory store outlets on your back-to-school and spring/summer shopping list. They start getting fall goods around mid-July; through mid-August, you can figure on a 30%–40% reduction off the regular retail price. Consistent in their quality designs, you can count on Hartstrings for beautifully detailed kilts, jumpers, jackets, novelty sweaters, pants, polo shirts, toggle and European-styled, full-fashion wool coats. Springtime collections feature pastel cardigans, khaki and floral shorts, gingham skirts and jumpers, white cotton blouses with scalloped edging or appliqué trim, matching accessories and even bathing suits for Summer. Further reductions are taken as the seasons progress, down as far as 25% off already reduced hangtag prices. This is how kids should look, and this is what their clothes should cost.

Jeanne Mac's Factory Stores
Route 30
Townsend, VT 05353
(802) 365-7040

Hours: Mon.–Sun. 10–5:30 in season
Payment: AmEx, Visa, MC, checks
Phone orders accepted

You'll find the complete Jeanne Mac collection spanning all the seasons from this company's famous line of 100% cotton playwear for boys and girls at savings ranging from 40%–70% off retail prices. They have lots of air-brushed, garment-dyed dresses and fleece-lined sweatshirts and sweat pants in dozens of fun prints. All garments are pre-shrunk—so wash away! If you're not in the Vermont area, give them a call and tell them what you need and they'll be pleased to mail-order their terrific bargains directly to your home. Call to check whether the factory stores are open. Hours vary, especially in Winter. Take note of their varying hours—in the Winter. Jeanne Mac is open Fri., Sat., Sun. and Mon.; however, from Memorial Day right into foliage, they are open seven days a week.

JM Originals
Factory Front Room Store
Berme Road
Box 628
Ellenville, NY 12428
Mail/phone orders accepted
(914) 647-1111 or (914) 647-3003

Hours: Mon.–Sun. 10–5
Payment: Major credit cards, checks

A favorite among competitive bargain hunters, you'll find some of the most fashion-forward collections at this warehouse/factory store.
If you're planning a trip to the resorts in the Catskills, make sure to include JM as one of your main activities in between the feeding frenzies. JM puts out several lines each season to accommodate all tastes, so whether you're a lover of bejeweled ornamentation or more sophisticated looks, they'll probably have something to suit your taste. They always have plenty of leggings, and thermal and sweat separates on hand to help you fill in the basics. As for prices, figure on paying around 40% off in-season and up to 75% off out-of-season. Folks love JM so much, they plan their vacations around it and buy in bulk for the coming school year. If you can't get there, don't fret. Simply visit your local kids clothing hot spot and look through the JM goods. Jot down style numbers, or just make sure you can accurately describe the outfit you want on the phone. Have your child try on the garments to verify proper sizing, then call the above numbers and order away!

Just Imagine
Off-Price Store
800 N. Bedford Rd.
Mt. Kisco, NY 10549
(914) 666-2201

Payment: Visa, MC

Come to this funky red barn for fabulous outer wear and rain gear by Galapagos at wholesale prices and under. If your kids love those authentic-looking fireman coats complete with reflective safety tape, nobody does them better than Galapagos. Find them here in sizes 2T–16 at 50% off and lower. Lots of heavy sherpa pile, polar fleece, anoraks, flannel shirts, pants and peacoats too! For the femme fatale in your group, designer Francy is featured in sizes 4–14. Dresses, chenille sweaters and liquid lycra are in abundance at half off retail. Only 45 minutes from NYC.

K & R Warehouse Sales
602 West Branch Street
Spring Hope, NC 27882
(919) 478-3173

Payment: Cash

This warehouse opens its doors to the public twice a year, selling off Isabella dresses, Isabella bathing suits and Kate Greenaway dresses starting at 50% off retail to way below wholesale. The sales always take place right before Easter and just in time for back-to-school. The company places an ad detailing the sales events in two local North Carolina newspapers. Other than that, they don't have a mailing list, so you'll need to call them for exact dates and time. You'll find all sizes here from infant up to size 16.

Kids Are Magic
Off-Price Store
2293 Broadway
New York City (between 82nd & 83rd Sts.), NY 10024
(212) 875-9240

Hours: Mon., Tues., Wed. 10–7;
Thurs., Fri., Sat. 10–9;
Sun. 10–7
Payment: Major credit cards

This store did more than ruffle a few retail feathers on the Upper West Side when it opened this 7,000-square-foot, two-story, bargain hunter's paradise! Impressive brand-name merchandise for boys and girls including Rothschild coats and Sahara Club are here at drastically reduced prices. On a recent expedition I noticed lovely dresses for as low as $17. Two days later I spotted the same brand at Lord & Taylor for $46! Where would you rather go? Now cashing in on the private label act, they are producing quality tights available to consumers for $2.99; comparable Trimfits would go for around $8. This is the place to stock up on pajamas, boy's school pants, blazers, socks and backpacks.

Kids Clothing Factory Outlet Stores
143 East Merrick Road
Freeport, NY 11520
(516) 378-3600 or fax:
(516) 378-3624

Call for an appointment
Phone orders accepted

Here's a terrific opportunity to purchase those adorable Baby Amore nylon jogging sets seen at Neiman-Marcus and other fine department stores at wholesale prices. They have recently extended their outerwear line to include outrageously cute, polar fleece-lined, vinyl, hooded anorak jackets, trimmed with faux leopard and Persian lamb. Find them here for $60; regular retail would set you back around $100! Other notably discounted items include their lycra/acetate legging and coordinated swing top with rosette trim. Hats are another recent addition here, featuring velvet and velour floppy, granny and baseball caps. Plenty of jogging sets are on hand for $10–$21. Most sizes are available from 12 months to 14 years. Out-of-towners can call and place their orders by phone or fax. If you're a local, call first and set up an appointment.

Kids Plus Discount Stores
70 Route 10
Whippany, NJ 07981
(201) 386-1005

Hours: Mon.–Sat. 10–5
Payment: Visa, MC, checks

What's the plus for? Savings! Some solid brands here for boys and girls in sizes newborn to 18 at everyday discounts of 25% and up. A frequent buyer's program is offered here where they tally up your annual sales and reward you with gift certificates. Here are some of the outstanding labels found at Kids Plus: Nicole Miller, Plum Pudding, Cary, Esprit, Cavaricci, Stamp, City Lights, Hartstrings, Awesome Graphics, JM Originals, Guess, Flap-doodles, My Michelle and so much more.

Knitwaves Outlet Stores
12 Empire Blvd.
Moonachie, New Jersey 07074
(201) 440-6890

Hours: Mon.–Fri. 8:30–4:00
Payment: Visa, MC

The design team at Knitwaves really seems to have a sense of what girls want, from retro looks to colorful twirly cheerleader skirts and matching sweaters. The outlet store will not quote prices on the phone; however, you can be assured of a reasonable discount (40% off retail) on current and past-season goods. They carry both Knitwaves and Miniwaves in sizes 2T–16 years. Although predominantly a girls line, we have seen some sweaters for boys (Jurassic Park) in the past at low prices too! By the way, this is New Jersey, so there's no sales tax on clothing.

Les Touts Petits Seasonal Warehouse Sales
600 Grand Ave
Ridgefield, NJ 07657
(201) 941-8675

These are strictly warehouse sales. Once you're on the mailing list, you'll get postcards alerting you to the dates and hours of the sales.

Boy, do the retailers hate this one! You'll find this line in better boutiques at prices only a Trump can afford, well at least I can't (won't) pay $40 and up for a pair of velour leggings. But I would pay half of that, which is why I wait for their spectacular warehouse sales and buy in assorted sizes and colors. In the past, sales have taken place during the following months: September, February, May, December and June. Sales are held contingent upon the number of leftovers, overruns, returns etc. During the summer sales I stock up on their outstanding bathing suits made of superior lycra-blend fabrics in the most fashion-forward silhouettes. This is a great place to pick up camp wear with shorts and t-shirts going for around $5. These warehouse sales are a little difficult to predict; however, they do have a mailing list that will alert you to all sales throughout the year. The majority of the sales seem to take place during the week. My personal strategy is to get there as soon as the doors open, usually around 10; that way I'm out and back to pick my child up from school with time to spare.

A word of caution here—the sizes tend to run on the small side. To avoid problems, bring pants and shirts from your child's closet to compare for accurate fit. No charges and no kids allowed at this one. Oh, by the way, when you call, don't be discouraged if they tell you to look in your local retailers for the line. Tell them you will, but to kindly inform you of the next sale and add your name to the mailing list. Politeness will help get you the discounts you are seeking.

Lilykins, Johnnykins, Babekins Warehouse Sales
Burlington, VT 05401
(802) 862-9619

Mailer will give the address, hours and payment accepted at the off-site warehouse location.

You can depend on two warehouse sales a year from this comprehensive children's line that manufactures 100% cotton playwear and formal dresses in sizes infant to 14. During their September and April sales you'll be able to purchase these brightly colored and whimsical rompers, bloomies, shorts and t-shirt sets, sun dresses, pants, and special-occasion velveteen dress wear at 40%–70% off retail prices.

First-quality, current merchandise will be available at the sales. Johnnykins is the boys line and Babekins features bibs, drool cloths, towels and receiving blankets. Add your name to the mailing list by calling the above phone number and you'll receive notification of the next warehouse sale.

Little Marcy's Off-Price Family Department Store
66th Street & Bergenline Avenue
West New York, NJ 07093
(201) 861-2050

Hours: Mon.–Wed. and Sat., 10–6; Thurs. and Fri. 10–9; Sun. 12–5
Payment: Discover, Visa, and checks

If your kids want the fashion statements and it's you who must deal with the financial statements, then head over to this shopper's paradise for deep discounts on upscale brand names. Not for the conservative at heart, Little Marcy's specializes in clothes that stand out in a crowd from such companies as Beverly Hills Kids, Romantic Bebe, Baby Amore, Zoe, Tom Kid, Zoodles, Baby Lulu, Wes & Willy, Monsterwear, Tag Rag, Three Wishes, Tickle Me!, JM Originals and more. Figure on 30% to 50% reductions off manufacturer-suggested prices. This store gets our stamp of approval based on competitive prices and immense inventory. Free parking on Sundays—otherwise there is metered parking around the store, which is not always easy to get, however.

Little Me Factory Store
47 Baltimore St.
Cumberland, MD 21502
(301) 722-5636

Hours: Call—the store is new and hours haven't been set yet. Phone orders ok!

Jeepers creepers, here's where to buy those beautiful Little Me creepers at discount prices! If you're at all familiar with the Little Me line, then you know how outstanding the design and tailoring are! Find current goods in sizes premie to 24 months in stretchalls, playwear, gowns and creepers starting at 20% off first-quality merchandise. Little Me Sports for toddlers up to size 4T is also here in short sets, T-shirts, pantsets and other basics. Ralph Lauren for infants up to size 7 is available starting at 20% off retail. Past-season goods, closeouts, irregulars and samples of both lines are also featured at up to 60% off retail!

Loli Of Vermont
On-Site Factory Store
71 North Main Street
St. Albans, VT 05478
(802) 527-1632

Hours: Mon.–Sat. 10–5
Payment: Checks, no credit cards
Mail/phone orders accepted

Don't "Loli-gag" about calling or visiting this on-site factory outlet shop where you can purchase top-quality cotton/lycra playwear and swimwear for boys and girls size 6 months to 14 years, at 50%–85% off suggested retail prices. Featured in such upscale catalogs as Garnet Hill, parents love Loli's for their solid construction and whimsical, exclusive prints. They have recently assembled a free color catalog that can assist you in your treasure hunt for bargains. We were particularly fond of the infant flight caps with adjustable velcro closure, retail $12, here for $5; baby doll dresses, retail $48, here for $24 and coordinated banana bandana leggings, retail $18, here for $9 with matching bow-beret. Lots of bodysuits, tunic tops, fleece and knit trousers for boys, vests, turtlenecks, bike shorts and jams. Loli's holds two blow-out clearances a year from January–March and August–October. Most merchandise consists of first-quality overruns; however, they do manufacture certain items expressly for the outlet shop from discontinued and leftover fabrics. St. Albans is located in the northwestern part of Vermont, which is 30 minutes outside of Burlington and Montreal. If you can't visit in person, you have to call; after all, every kid deserves a Loli.

Magic Moments
Good Lad Factory Stores
431 E. Tioga Street
Philadelphia, PA 19134
(215) 739-2237

Red Lion Rd. and Bustleton Ave.
Philadelphia, PA 19115
(215) 671-1694

Rockvale Square Outlets
Store 409
Lancaster, PA 17602
(717) 293-1924

Reading Outlet Center
801 N. 9th Street
Reading, PA 19604
(610) 373-5303

Franklin Mills Mall
Green Zone
Franklin Mills, PA 19114
(215) 281-3299

Payment: Visa, MC

The store name may be Magic Moments, but the merchandise is Good Lad. If you love traditional and classic looks for your lads and lassies size 7 and under, then this is for you. (Order the Olsen's Mill Direct catalog at (800) 452-3699 and see the line for yourself.) Lots of pretty plaids, flannel dresses with matching leggings, party dresses, nautical looks and a full supply of accessories including headbands, hats, bows, socks, gloves and mittens. Grandma will swoon when she sees the boys in their velvet knickers, shirt and bow-tie sets, or the basic pants, sweaters and vests. The prices are magic at 40% below retail and the merchandise is current.

Marden's Surplus and Salvage Stores
(207) 873-6111 (call this main number for 7 Maine locations)

Hours: Mon.–Fri. 9–8; Sat. 9–5; Sun. 12–5
Payment: Visa, MC, Discover

Here's a unique operation. This company buys up first-quality overstocks and closeouts, and salvages inventory by bidding on lots of merchandise that has been involved in hurricanes, earthquakes, tornadoes, you name it! The result is big savings for you on almost anything! Marden's claims to have seen most kid clothing lines, branded and private label, pass through the doors at some point in time over their 30 years in business. Expect to reap average discounts of 40% to 70% off retail prices.

Marsha Inc. Factory Outlet Store
32 Tioga Way
Marblehead, MA 01945
(617) 631-5511

Hours: Mon.–Fri. 10–4
Payment: Checks
Catalog and mail orders accepted

This is a popular collection found in fashion-forward boutiques that make the girls go gaga. Rhinestone, lace and appliqué designs on thermal tops, t-shirts, denim and dresses, plus matching leggings are here at 40% below retail and more when you scrounge through their bins and damage racks. If you live near or plan on visiting Boston, stop by this outlet store and you'll find showroom samples and irregulars. For first-quality, current goods, expect to pay a few dollars above wholesale. They have all sizes from 6 months to 14 years.

Millie's Sillies
87 Roundhill Road
Armonk, NY 10504
(914) 273-1817

Payment: Cash only

There's nothing silly about the low, wholesale and below prices at these biannual warehouse sales of the most exquisite girls' dress accessories featured in one of the most upscale children's fashion catalogs. If you call the above phone number, you'll be placed on the mailing list and will receive notification of upcoming warehouse sales. (On occasion, they sell some high-ticket boys and girls lines at wholesale and below prices in conjunction with their own merchandise at the sales.) You'll find plenty of satin, ballet flats with bows, pearl, rhinestone and floral accents; satin rosette headbands; little-lady, mesh gloves; be-ribboned, floral halos; tulle-net hairbows and novelty purses. (These floral halos look great simply hanging in a little girl's room. I just stuck a thumbtack in a bulletin board and hung the halo on it. What a romantic look!)

Modern Kids Outlet Stores
73 Main Street
Phoenicia, NY 12464
(914) 688-7226

Hours: Thurs.–Mon. 9–5
Free brochure and mail/phone orders accepted

For your thoroughly modern minis, get to know Modern Kids! The all-time hippest pair of leggings my child ever wore were made by this ultra-stylish manufacturer of "action wear" separates. What I didn't know at the time was that I could've called up the outlet store and ordered them over the phone at half of what I ended up paying in some ritzy little boutique I didn't want to be in the first place! Modern Kids produces the best-fitting and funkiest prints by using the most expensive inks and high-quality cotton/lycra combinations. All sizes here, from infant up through preteen 14. You can purchase Modern Kids overruns (first quality), closeouts and samples at wholesale prices at the outlet store in Phoenicia, New York. Or, just call or write for the brand-new brochure and order over the phone.

Mona's Kids
Off-Price Stores
477 Bellmore Avenue
East Meadow, NY 11554
(516) 483-4577

1310 N. University Drive
Coral Springs, FL 33071
(305) 346-0805

8177 Glades Road
Boca Raton, FL 33433
(407) 852-8588

Payment: Visa, MC
Phone orders accepted

Samples on Long Island, New York and southern Florida? Can it be? What a terrific find for all of you fashion-conscious parents, grandparents and friends who can't get to the children's design buildings for showroom samples. Mona's has one-of-a-kind samples from the most innovative children's collections at 50% off retail prices. The beauty of this off-price store is two-fold. First, prices on samples are unbeatable, and second, the buyers' taste is impeccable. (It's quite difficult to find "Hollywood Babe—Call My Agent" at wholesale prices, but here they are!) In addition to the samples, the stores also carry regular stock items at 25% off or more at all times. The all-star cast here includes Hollywood Babe—Call My Agent (that three piece number on the cover of this book, the dress, bolero jacket and matching hat are all from Hollywood Babe), Wes & Willy, Hank Player, Tom Kid, Baby Boxers,Leggoons, Antique Boutique, Rubbies, Artwear By Halley, Bonnie & Clyde, My Boy Sam, Les Touts Petits and many other co-stars. The sales staff is very experienced and helpful. They'll even fulfill phone orders for out-of-towners who know what they want.

My Precious Rose
Off-Price Store
Sidewalk Sample Sales
170 Gravesend Avenue
Brooklyn, NY 11223
(718) 336-2335

Hours: Mon.–Fri. 10–7;
Sat. 10–6
Payment: Major credit cards

You may already be familiar with the beautifully embellished Janet-Baby infant and layette line, but what you probably don't know is that Janet herself operates a discount children's store selling off sample and stock merchandise throughout the year. Here's how it works: In warm weather the store moves outside for their sidewalk sales and sells off Janet's samples along with samples from other vendors. The sales begin around May and continue through Fall. Some of the lines available to consumers at up to 90% off retail prices include Kathy's Clown, Tickle Me!, JM Originals, Golden Rainbow and of course, Janet-Baby. If you need a baby gift, this must be the place! Sizes are limited here, going up to 4T in boys and size 7 in girls.

Natan Borlam
Off-Price Store
152 Havermeyer Street
Brooklyn, NY 11211
(718) 782-0108

Hours: Sun.–Thurs. 10–5;
Fri. 10–2
Payment: Checks (Visa and MC on phone orders)
Phone orders accepted

This wholesaler of better childrens wear has been around for over 35 years keeping local kids on the "best-dressed" list in schools around the Tri-State area. Now "Mr. B," (as we alumni affectionately call him) is happy to fill phone orders from around the country. They don't have a catalog, so you have to know exactly what you want. Borlam's offers imported, boutique-line dresses, suits, blazers and outerwear at up to 60% off regular retail. You'll consistently find such designer names and brands as Rothschild coats, Jonathan Stone, Francois Bouthillier, Magil, Sylvia Whyte, Isabel Garreton, Mousefeathers, Robin International coats, Jean Bourget, Gottex bathing suits, Knitwaves, Giesswien boiled wool jackets/cardigans, Clayeux, Boston Traders and more. I like to browse through the better department stores that carry these upscale lines, make mental notes of the prices and then head over to Borlam's to play the numbers. And with a little persistent haggling, you may get a few extra dollars taken off the regular discounted price—especially if you're making multiple purchases. The neighborhood here is not the greatest (remember, low rents mean bigger savings), but they do have a parking lot across the street for customers only.

Nina Shoe Outlet
27–01 Queens Blvd.
Long Island City, NY 11101
(718) 784-0519

Hours: Mon.–Fri. 9–4:30;
Sat. 10–6
Payment: Most major credit cards

I'll never forget the most elegant pair of shoes my mother bought for me at Bergdorf Goodman when I was ten years old. They were composed of glove-soft, navy leather and had a bow-trimmed ankle strap. Hard-pressed to find anything comparable today, I was thrilled to learn about the Nina Doll shoe group that boasts similar designs. The outlet shop in Long Island City purchases surplus shoes and boots from the kids division of Nina's shoes and sells them off at 30% to 50% off department store prices. These well-constructed and flattering styles include dressy and school-appropriate T-straps, slip-ons, velvets, boots, sandals and more.

Old Navy
(800) 653-6289

Call for the location near you and specials of the week. Payment and return information also available on the recording.

Here's a terrific shopping resource for the whole family, courtesy of the Gap. These lower-priced cotton and some poly/cotton blends are featured in surprisingly high-styled silhouettes. Special promotions and selections of the week bring prices down further. For example, one of my favorite summer promotions highlighted a beautiful, white cotton, embroidered dirndl skirt for $7! Shortalls at Old Navy go for around $18; you'd have to shell out almost twice that at a regular Gap store! Regular jeans go for about $15 and low-top sneakers can be had for about $9! I especially love their wide, stretch cotton and lycra headbands (a lifesaver if your daughter has decided to let her bangs grow out), in assorted colors at $2 apiece.

Patagonia Outlet Store
#9 Bo Street
Freeport, ME 04032
(207) 865-0506

Hours: Mon.–Sat. 9–9;
Sun. 10–7
Payment: Visa, MC, Discover, AmEx and checks
Catalog and mail orders accepted

Pat yourself on the back for finding a way to obtain these exclusive, outdoor sporting clothes at 30% off and better. Order the catalog and give yourself an education on the sporting life and the obligatory wardrobe, then visit one of their four outlets in the U.S. (see Salt Lake City, UT; Dillon, MT; and Ventura, CA). If you call the outlet, the sales staff will eagerly inform you of weekly bargain specials, or if you prefer, they will fax the list to you. Sizes start at 3 months (try the Synchilla bunting—their trademark polar fleece) and go up to size 14. We've been told that clothes from Patagonia make it through about anything—and are extremely functional. The folks at Patagonia also seem to be the experts at keeping your kids warm during the coldest of outdoor activities, from mountain climbing to skiing. Gift certificates are available.

Patsy Aiken Company Stores
4812 Hargrove Road
Raleigh, NC 27604
(919) 872-8789

Cotswold Mall
300-CS
Charlotte, NC 28211
(704) 365-3723

Payment: MC, Visa

When my daughter was little, this was a favorite in our house. Bright, cheerful cotton or poly/cotton sportswear, playwear, swimwear and layette trimmed with darling appliqué and embroidery. This is strictly for whippersnappers size infant–6X. If you go directly to the store you'll find reductions ranging from 15%–60% below retail throughout the year. In January and June, however, they hold one of the South's most popular "attic" sales where everything is cleared out at cost prices. Get yourself on their mailing list for announcements of seasonal promotions and sales.

Quiltex Outlet Store
168 39th Street
Brooklyn, NY 11232
(718) 788-3158

Hours: Mon.–Thurs. 8–4;
Fri. 8–1
Payment: Visa, MC, AmEx
No checks

There is free parking for customers at 3901 1st Avenue.

Why bother registering at the retail baby stores for layette and bedding when you can go directly to the Quiltex factory store and save a bundle for your bundle? Everything for babies, including stretchies, sweaters, snowsuits, bedding and decorative gifts is available here at wholesale prices and way below.

Richie's Shoes
Off-Price Shoes
183 Avenue B (between 11th and 12th Sts.)
New York, NY 10009
(212) 228-5442

Hours: 10–5 daily; closed on Wed.
Payment: Visa, MC, AmEx, checks
Mail-order/phone orders accepted

Perhaps your biggest fashion dilemma is finding better-quality shoes at discount prices. Richie and family have run this small but well-stocked off-price shoe store for the past 80 years. You'll find the following brands at 20% to 40% below department store prices: Baby Botte (no kidding!), Enzo, Rachels (the perfect party dress accompaniment), Jonathan B (my personal favorite), Tretorn, Bass, Eastland,

Keds and more. Richie is most accommodating and won't let you walk out of the store with a pair of shoes unless it's a perfect fit. If you know exactly what you want and the right size, Richie will ship anywhere in the country. He also suggests that customers call first to make sure that he has what they need. He doesn't believe in wasting anyone's time.

Simi Factory Stores
One Lyme Common
Lyme, NH 03768
(603) 795-4359

Hours: Mon.–Sat. 8:15–4
Payment: MC, Visa, checks
Phone/mail orders accepted

Here's a line of superior-quality dresswear for boys and girls that can be seen in Neiman-Marcus and Nordstrom. Lots of velvet, taffeta and corduroy, European tea-length frocks for the girls (size 3 months–preteen) and knickers for the boys (only up to size 4T). Their warm-weather collections consist of summer-weight dresses and shorts. The beauty of Simi dresses lies in their die-fast fabrics, which allow you to machine-wash most of the garments over and over without fear of fading. Everyday prices at the outlets guarantee a 30% discount off the department store hangtags (not the sale tags). Compound these reductions with Simi's end-of-season sales and you'll save between 60%–75% off retail prices. If you see something you like in the department stores, copy down the style numbers, select a size/color and you can order by calling the San Marcos, Texas outlet store at (512) 353-3042; 3939 IH 35 South, Suite 131, San Marcos, TX.

So Fun Kids Outlets
Millstream Factory Outlets
306 Outlet Drive
Lancaster, PA 17602-1467
(717) 393-4432

Krewstown Shopping Center
9315 Krewstown Road
Philadelphia, PA 19115
(215) 464-6626

St. Augustine Outlet Center
2700 State Road 16
Suite 1003
St. Augustine, FL 32084
(904) 824-8698

Riviera Centre Factory Store
2601 Kenzie Street
Foley, AL 36535
(334) 943-3271

Penn's Purchase Factory Outlet Village
Bldg. C Shop #1
5861 York Road
Lahaska, PA 18931
(215) 794-2791

1755 Ocean Outlets
Rehoboth Beach, DE 19971
(302) 226-9888

The Outlets at Vero Beach
1744 94th Drive
Space G190
Vero Beach, FL 32966
(407) 564-0360

Myrtle Beach Factory Stores
4633 Hwy. 501
Space C160
Myrtle Beach, SC 29577
(803) 236-5403

Ocean City Factory Stores
12641 Ocean Gateway
Space 208
Ocean City, MD 29577
(410) 213-1135

So excited? You should be. This vibrantly colored line of top-quality, cotton/lycra active wear carried in specialty boutiques around the country is now available at 30% off and more at the outlet stores. A lot of parents compare So Fun! to Flapdoodles; however, in my opinion, I don't believe they're comparable. Their designs, color palette and needlework get higher marks in my book.

Strasburg Lace Outlets
Riviera Outlet
2601 Kensie
Foley, AL 36530
(334) 943-7111

3070 Leeman Ferry Rd.
Huntsville, AL 35801
(205) 880-2040

401 Elizabeth Street
Boaz, AL 35957
(205) 593-2274

Free catalog and phone/mail orders accepted

For special-occasion dressing at 40% to 60% off retail, these handsewn, embroidered dresses in silk, chiffon, organdy and organza are as close as I've seen to antique-type, heirloom creations in the 1990s. Little boys are not forgotten here, with knickers, short pants and coordinating smocked cotton tops, making them look oh so princely! Christening gowns, bonnets and hair accessories are also available. Call for your free color catalog, provide them with your child's measurements and the store promises you a perfect fit! Discounted merchandise is shipped anywhere in the United States.

Teddy Bears by the Seashore Off-Price Store
1306 Third Ave.
Spring Lakes, NJ 07762
(908) 449-9013

Hours: Mon.–Sun. 11–4
Payment: Visa, MC, checks

This shop in Spring Lakes, NJ (nicknamed the Irish Riviera) offers 30%–60% off at all times on traditional and classic dressing for boys and girls. If you're looking for boys' velvet knickers and traffic-stopping ball gowns for girls, this must be the place. They also stock a large inventory of better smocked dresses. In the past we've spotted such elegant lines as Anne Savoy, Vive La Fete, Rosey's Kids, Cary, and Wee Clancy.

Therese's Collection Biannual Warehouse Sales
301 Nott Street
Schenectady, NY 12305
(518) 346-2315

Payment: Visa, MC, checks

Shhhh! This one's a really big secret. I told you that we'd divulge the sources of those high-ticket kid clothing catalogs. These designers and manufacturers of classic, traditional and specialty mother/daughter/sister, mother/son ensembles open their doors to the public twice a year to sell off leftovers, overruns and samples at 60% below catalog prices. Oh, what catalog, you ask? The very upscale and pricey Wooden Soldier. The sales always take place before Thanks-giving and Easter. So, what you need to do is call up and get on the mailing list, or simply ask for the exact dates of the next blow-out sale. You'll find all sizes for girls from 6 months to 14 and boys up to size 7. Always double-check on payment policy before making the trip.

Tickle Me! Totally Me! Tackle Me! Backroom Factory Store & Warehouse Clearances
33–20 48th Ave.
Long Island City, NY 11101
(718) 392-9215

Hours: Mon.–Fri. 10–3
Payment: Visa, MC, no checks
Cash only at warehouse sales

Mercy me! This is one of the more outstanding kid lines in the industry with numerous fashion awards under their creative belt to prove it, including the coveted Earnshaw's design award. On the retail level, this stuff doesn't come cheap, but you can visit their store at the factory in Long Island City and the line becomes very affordable at wholesale prices and way below. Make sure to put your name on their mailing list to be notified of warehouse events throughout the year when prices drop even further. They will provide you with a large box with a string handle attached which you drag around and fill with goodies. A word of caution: People go nuts at these sales, running here and there and grabbing everything in sight. Watch your feet! It's easy to get tangled up in the strings and trip over the boxes. Also, if you love your kids, leave them at home—it's just too dangerous here (steep staircases, etc.).

Tommy Hilfiger Outlet Stores Warehouse Sale
112 Truman Street
Edison, NJ 08818
(908) 572-1888

Rehoboth Outlet Center
4565 Highway #1
Rehoboth Beach, DE 19971
(302) 645-4990

Magnolia Bluff Factory Shops
1 Magnolia Bluff Way
Darien, GA 31305
(912) 437-2808

Worcester Common Fashion Outlet
100 Front Street
Worcester, MA 01608
(508) 767-1400

The Maine Outlets
345 US Rt. 1
Kittery, ME 03904
(207) 439-8880

Ocean City Factory Outlets
12741 Ocean Gate Way
Ocean City, MD 21842
(410) 213-8200

180 Herrod Blvd.
Dayton, NJ 08810
(609) 860-9700

Liberty Village Factory Outlet
76 Liberty Village
Flemington, NJ 08822
(908) 782-1150

Woodbury Common III
Route 32
Central Valley, NY 10917
(914) 928-8888

French Mountain Commons
Route 9
Lake George, NY 12845
(518) 743-1880

Niagara Falls Outlet Mall
1744 Military Rd.
Niagara Falls, NY 14304
(716) 298-8888

Tanger Factory Outlet
1770 W. Main Street
Riverhead, NY 11901
(516) 369-0050

Designer's Place—Vanity Fair
739 Reading Ave.
Reading, PA 19611
(610) 372-8777

Reading Outlet Center
831 Oley Street
Reading, PA 19604
(610) 371-8880

Rockvale Square
35 S. Willowdale Dr.
Lancaster, PA 17602
(717) 399-8888

Crossings Factory Stores
285 Crossings Outlet Square
Tannersville, PA 18372
(717) 688-9888

Manchester Square
Rt. 11 & Rt. 30
Manchester, VT
(802) 362-0888

Boy oh boy, if you've got a boy then this one's for you! Year-round you can count on discounts of 30%–35% off regular retail prices. They claim to be either one season behind or one year later. However, our experience has taught us that one season behind for outlets is right in season for you and me! Find even greater reductions after holidays and toward the end of the "real" season. All boys sizes here start from toddler and go on up to grandpa! The company also hosts an annual warehouse sale whose location varies from year to year. Call the Edison, New Jersey phone number for the exact location. The sale traditionally takes place in December. Do not miss it! Hilfiger isn't the only one who can "figer" out a good thing!

Tuesdays Too!
1429 Coney Island Avenue
(between Ave J & K)
Brooklyn, NY 11230
(718) 338-7022

Hours: Mon.–Fri. and Sun 10:30–7
Payment: Visa, MC, AmEx, checks

How would you like to pay 70% off retail prices all year round on the finest European children's clothing? This warehouse is the final destination for inventory from the very upscale Tuesday's Child Boutique in Brooklyn, NY. The warehouse receives shipments from the retail store at the end of each season and there they remain, marked down to 70% below retail until some lucky shopper grabs up the bargains. We want that lucky someone to be you! The store owners also buy up closeouts throughout the year and deposit them in the warehouse. You'll find a galaxy of star designers here including Simonetta, Sonia Rykiel, Ozona, Clayeux, New Man, Maugin, Florian, Cachelle, Baby Graziella, Magil, Pappa & Ciccia, Paper Moon, Kinder, Marese and more at very affordable prices. All sizes for boys and girls from newborn to 20.

Wholesale For Kids Closeout Specialty Stores
8 locations in New Jersey:
Old Bridge—(908) 679-9090
Sayreville—(908) 525-0733
Lakewood—(908) 370-4900
Shrewsbury—(908) 747-1900
Bricktown—(908) 295-1300
Freehold—(908) 780-0007
Matawan—(908) 566-9488
Seaview—(908) 918-1211

This is strictly a hit-or-miss situation. However, we bring it to your attention for the fabulous buys you can sometimes pick up. These are mid-priced lines with a few designers sprinkled in from time to time. These stores are a great source for play clothes, camp basics, sleep wear, Halloween costumes and bathing suits at wholesale and below prices. I've even seen Rothschild and Young Gallery outerwear at unheard-of sticker prices. Normal reductions here are 40% to 60% off retail. However, they take further reductions, 50% off wholesale, at the end of each season and host their famous "Midnight Madness" sales four times a year, where an additional 20% off all merchandise is deducted resulting in give-'em-away" prices! Once again, they're from Jersey and there is no sales tax.

Wooden Soldier Outlet
Kearsage St.
North Conway Village, NH 03860
(603) 356-5643

Hours: Mon.–Sat. 9–9; Sun. 10–5
Payment: Major credit cards, checks

Route 16
Intervale, NH 03845

Hours: Mon.–Sat. 9–5 (6:30 in Summer); Sun. 10–5

You've read the catalog (available by calling 800 375 6002), now see the outlet stores! For special-occasion dresing (especially if you love those brother/sister, mother/daughter and mother/daughter/son looks), this is the place! You'll find velvet knickers for the little Lord Fauntleroy in your clan, hand-smocked dresses, Little Bo-Peep, fairytale frocks and more. The outlet stores feature leftover and past-season merchandise from the Wooden Soldier catalogs. Prices start at 30% below catalog prices and increase in relation to the age of the goods. Two tent sales are held in the summer when reductions can be as much as 80% off catalog prices.

Southern Region

Chocolate Soup Discount Store
46 Town & Country Road
Houston, TX 77024
(713) 467-5957
(816) 525-2222 for a store location near you

There are sweet savings at any of the 14 stores in the South, Midwest and as far west as Colorado. This company manufactures its own brand of moderate to better childrenswear for their stores exclusively. By eliminating the middleman, great savings are passed on to you. Other brands carried in the stores include Oshkosh, Eagles Eye, Le Top, Nautica, Rosey Kids, Good Lad, Imp, Baby Togs and lots more at 20% off and more depending on the specific sale. End of season sales cansee reductions go as high as 60% off; however, discounts can vary greatly here. You'll find sizes infant–14 for girls and infant-size 7 for boys.

House of Hatten Outlet Store
3939 1H-35 Suite 725
San Marcos, TX 78666
(512) 392-8161

Hours: Mon.–Sat. 10–9; Sun 11–6
Payment: Visa, MC, AmEx, Discover, checks
Phone orders accepted

Every baby and child needs an heirloom-quality something, whether it's a hand-smocked romper, bonnet or keepsake bunny, and every parent shouldn't have to take out a second mortgage to pay for it! Enter the House of Hatten outlet store, which will be happy to ship anywhere in the U.S., provided you know what you want. You'll find exquisite, albeit traditional, appliquéd and embroidered dresses, bubbles, shirts, sun dresses, jumpsuits, hats, bibs, bunting, rattles and more at 30% off and higher during end-of-season sales. Most merchandise found here is discontinued, imperfect or damaged. This outlet is for the wee ones, size newborn to 4T only.

Liberty & Duck Head Outlet Store
3500 Fifth Avenue South
Birmingham, AL 35222
(205) 251-7038

Hours: Mon.–Fri. 9–4:30; Sat. 9–4
Payments: MC, Visa, checks

This outlet store carries irregulars from Liberty and Duck Head for kids. You'll find very affordable prices on both lines; however, the Liberty collection goes to only size 4T. Duck Head for boys and girls starts at size 12 months and goes up to size 16. We love their adorable appliquéd and pleated bib overalls for girls. Plenty of casual khaki pants, striped polo shirts, zipped cotton-knit tops and henleys for boys.

Small Fry Off-Price Store
330 Sunset
Denton, TX (near Dallas/ Fort Worth) 76201
(817) 387-9915

Hours: Mon.–Sat 10–6
Payment: MC, Visa and Discover, checks
Phone orders accepted

Deep in the heart of Texas you can actually purchase samples at up to 60% off regular retail prices from such wonderful kid lines as Baby Guess, Guess, Cary, Dorissa, Monday's Child, Zoodles, Spumoni, Karavan, Melissa Jackson and more! If you can accurately describe what you want, they'll mail-order your requests. In the area? Swing by for big savings.

West Coast Region

After The Stork
Outlet Store
4411 San Mateo NE
Albuquerque, NM 87101
(505) 881-9630

Hours: Mon.–Sat. 10–8;
Sun 12–5
Payment: MC, Visa, checks

If you love the 100% organically grown cotton separates from the After The Stork catalog, then check out the outlet and catalog store for some major bargains. Lots of colorful basics, long johns, thermal knit onesies, fleece jackets, rompers, dresses (plaids and velour), pants, sweats, socks, hats and of course, diaper covers. Everyday discounts on year-old overstocks (still very current styles) come to about 30%–40% off retail with additional reductions taken throughout the year amounting to an extra 25% off already reduced goods. Take a peek at their separate catalog room where all current catalog merchandise is available at 10% off catalog prices. Gift certificates are available for an interesting gift idea.

Biobottoms
Outlet Stores
Catalog
620 Petaluma Blvd.
Suite H
Petaluma, CA 49452
(707) 778-1948

Hours: Mon.–Fri. 10–6;
Sat. 10–5
Payment: Visa, MC, AmEx, Discover, checks

Call (800) 766-1254 and order the Biobottoms catalog to familiarize yourself with the merchandise and prices, then head over to the factory store and save up to 50% on their extraordinarily well-made garments. Famous for their 100% wool diaper cover—the Biobottom—they also manufacture a Cotton Bottom made of cotton and polyester. The company claims that these cloth diaper covers are so well-constructed that you can actually hand them down from generation to generation! (Not that I'd want to.) For the older kids up through preteen, they've got plenty of casual wear, dresses (velour and cotton), pants, shirts and swimsuits in bright, cheerful colors and patterns. The goods are first-quality, current leftovers from the catalog sales department.

Biscotti
Seasonal Warehouse Sales
144 Linden Street (3rd Street)
Oakland, CA 94607
(510) 272-9122

Payment: Visa, MC

Romantic-looking dresses, separates, rompers and jumpsuits in delicate colors and fabrics by Biscotti can be bought at 30%–50% off retail and better, at their twice-a-year warehouse sale. Call up and put your name on the mailing list and they'll send a postcard alerting you to the exact dates and hours of the pre-Easter and pre-Christmas sales. Sizes here begin at nine months and go up to size 14.

Cary Outlet Store
2390 Fourth Street
Berkeley, CA 94710
(510) 841-5700

Hours: Mon.–Sat. 10–4:30
Payment: Visa, MC

You'll carry out great bargains for your grateful daughter from the Cary outlet. We've been following this line for several years and boy, I mean girl, have they grown! Cary started out specializing in girls' dresses; they now have Cary Sports-fleece tops, lycra leggings, woven skirts and pants; Cary Coats—wool dress coats, swing car coats, duffels with plaid flannel lining; Tini Kini-swimwear, bike shorts and playwear. Of course, their classic dresses consisting of cotton stripes, dot patterns, florals, seersuckers and plaid flannels for colder weather are still around, too! You'll find ultra-low prices on overruns and seconds (don't worry, seconds are marked), at wholesale and below. The store does enforce a strict return policy—there are none! So make sure whatever you choose is a keeper.

Christine Foley Factory Stores
430 Ninth Street
San Francisco, CA 94103
(415) 621-8126

Hours: Mon.–Sat. 10–4; Sun. 12–4
Payment: Visa, MC, checks

These very pricey, hand-loomed sweaters, found in the most upscale boutiques and department stores, are sold off at wholesale prices in this retail outlet shop. You can select from unique, discontinued patterns and purchase a hand–me–down-quality creation at a reasonable price. Christine Foley's philosophy holds that a child's life is full of fantasy and should be reflected in the clothes they wear. Foley's whimsical designs exemplify her convictions. You and the kids might be excited to know that many of the Foley sweaters have appeared on such prominent sitcoms as the Cosby Show (Bill and the Cosby kids donned the delightful sweaters) and thirtysomething (remember little Janie?). Expect to pay between $54 and $74 for kids' sweaters starting at toddler 2 and all the way up through adult sizes.

Creme de la Creme Outlet Stores
100 Citadel Drive
Suite 100
City Of Commerce, CA 90040
(213) 721-9392

2230 Mall Loop Rd. Unit 110
Lancaster, CA 93536
(805) 484-0829

740 E Ventura Blvd. Ste 226
Camarillo, CA 93010
(805) 945-6278

1300 Folsome Blvd. Ste 605
Folsome, CA 95630
(408) 842-2512

8375 Arroyo Circle Ste. 53
Gilroy, CA 75020
(916) 353-0137

2796 Tanger Way, Unit 203
Barstow, CA 92311
(619) 253-2506

17600 Collier Ave., Unit 142
Lake Elsinore, CA 92538
(909) 674-2884

Payment: All major credit cards

High-quality cottons and sophisticated designs are typical of this otherwise pricey playwear line for kids. You can purchase dresses, pants and rompers in sizes infant through 7 for boys, and infant through 6X for girls, at around 50% off retail prices in the outlet stores. Place yourself on their mailing list for advance sale notices and realize even better bargains.

Donna Capozzi Outlet Store
1005 Camelia Street
Berkeley, CA 94710
(510) 558-1100

Hours: Wed.– Sat. 10 – 5
Payment: Checks and cash only
Publications available: store mailer

I can't say enough great things about the European-inspired design and fabrics from this outstanding line of girls special-occasion and durable playwear. This one-and-only outlet for Capozzi sells off past-season outfits and separates at wholesale prices and below in sizes 12 months–preteen large. If you love tailored, refined silhouettes in linen and rayon fabrications, then this one's for you. Coordinating hair accessories, bows, scrunchies and hats also available.

Esse Pink
Weekly Warehouse Sale
2415 Third Street
Suite 231
San Francisco, CA 94107
(415) 255-6855

Hours: Generally Fri. 10–4
Payment: Cash only

Here's one of the more innovative children's clothing designers offering everything from size preemie jeans, (Eensie Esse), cooking and gardening duds (Essie Escapes) to their everyday sportswear-driven line for boys and girls size 6 months to 7 years. Once a week, Esse Pink opens its doors to the public, selling off end-of-season goods, overruns and irregulars at wholesale prices. However, they ask you to call first just to make sure they'll be there. Esse Pink is known for her attention to details and body shapes. (The gardening clothes have little messages on the pockets telling kids it's okay to get dirty.) Little girls love their Snow White silhouettes and moms love the blue plaid and white denim fabric they're made of. Lots of food themes here, especially vegetables! Pie prints even have steam coming out of the holes in the crust. The boys' line is actually designed in part by the owner's son, who sees to it that the line is terribly up to date with lots of rugged denim looks, outerwear, vests and trousers. If you know someone with a preemie, they should know that Eensie Esse has a full line of fashion-forward preemie clothes starting at size 2 1/2 pounds. Essie Pink hosts additional clearance sales two to three times a year and requests that you put your name on the mailing list so they can send you a flyer.

Flap Happy
Factory Store
1714 16th Street
Santa Monica, CA 90404
(800) 234-3527

Hours: Mon.–Sat. 10–5
Payment: MC, Discover, Visa, AmEx, checks

Looking for functional and adorable sun and winter hats for a baby? Then you should know about the Flap Happy hat designed specifically to protect the little one's delicate skin from the sun and harsh winter elements. If you've never seen them, think "Foreign Legion"—you know, the extra flap of material that comes off the hat to shade the nape of the neck and upper shoulders. The hat was originally produced in 100% cotton, but now comes in flannel, velvet and polar fleece. Flap Happy has recently expanded and now produces a clothing line for children from infant to size 7/8. The company has opened a new outlet store, selling off closeouts, over-orders, samples and seconds at wholesale prices and below. At the retail level these hats go for $10; at the outlet you can purchase three hats for $15. The store occasionally takes in over-runs and samples from other trendy manufacturers like Sweet Potatoes and Mullberribush, which are sold off at wholesale and below prices too. Place your name on the mailing list for notification of their twice-a-year blow-out sale where parents in the know line up early in the morning before the store opens to get first crack at the below-cost goods! The sale takes place before Christmas (great gifts) and in mid-July.

For Kids Only
Off-Price Stores
746 N. Fairfax
Los Angeles, CA 90046
(213) 650-4885

Hours: Mon.–Sat. 10–6;
Sun. 12–6

18332 Ventura Blvd.
Tarzana, CA 91356
(818) 708-9543

Hours: Mon.–Sat. 10–6;
Sun. 12–6
Payment: All major credit cards
Phone orders accepted

Where do many celebrity parents in Los Angeles shop for their nattily dressed offspring? For Kids Only specializes in high-style imports at 30%–70% off retail prices. You can make this a one-stop shopping destination by coordinating outfits with matching footwear. The owners of the store have impeccable buying taste, and you'll find many one-of-a kind items here. (They travel to Europe several times a year to make sure of it.) For Kids Only hosts an annual summer mid-July through mid-August) "Parking Lot" sale where already reduced items are marked down an additional 70%. If you can't get to the store, you can place orders over the phone.

Golden Rainbow & San Francisco Blues
435 A Brannan Street
San Francisco, CA 94107
(415) 543-5191

Hours: See sale flyers
Payment: See sale flyers

Somewhere over this "rainbow" lies a pot of "golden" savings for you and your kids. Call and place your name on their mailing list and they'll let you know when and where the warehouse sales will be. There doesn't seem to be any predictable schedule of sales, so you'll have to sit tight and wait for your postcard. Expect solid markdowns on their high-quality sweaters and sportswear in sizes up to 10 years. Their sale notice will tell you what form of payment they accept.

Hanna Andersson Factory Store
7 Monroe Parkway
Lake Oswego, OR
(503) 697-1953

Hours: Mon.–Fri. 10–6;
Sat. 10–5; Sun noon–5
Payment: AmEx, Visa, MC, Discover and checks
Phone orders accepted
(see Portsmouth, New Hampshire in East Coast region)

Call for the Hanna Andersson catalog at (800) 222-0544, then call this outlet store and they will be happy to ship your selections at a minimum reduction of 20% off catalog prices (reductions increase as the season progresses). The factory store receives past-season catalog items and sells them at 20%–40% discounts. **Bargain Bonus:** Remember to inquire about their ongoing road shows. If you're lucky enough to be visiting or actually live near a road show destination, make sure to attend these traveling blow-out sales, where Hanna's highly sought-after cotton kid clothes are reduced down to 50%–75% off catalog prices. Clearance sales are held 4–5 times a year, so call and get yourself on the mailing list for notification of precise dates.

Nathan J. Outlet Stores
17941 Brookshire Lane
Huntington Beach, CA 92647
(213) 725-1781

Hours: Mon.–Fri. 8–5
Payment: Most major credit cards

Nathan J. Outlet
100 Citadel Drive
Suite 104
City of Commerce, CA 90040
(800) 543-8465

Hours: Mon.–Sat 10–8;
Sun. 10–6

Good ol' reliable Nathan for your little guys and dolls. Nathan J. makes great-looking, great-fitting, 100% cotton underwear and layette for newborn up to size 4T. You can visit their showroom in Huntington Beach, where they'll let you choose from samples and then fetch whatever you need out of the warehouse. Prices here hover around wholesale. Or, you can go to the outlet store in City of Commerce. The outlet store has the additional feature of carrying other manufacturers at discounts of 30%–40% off retail prices. Some reputable lines carried by the outlet include Plum Pudding, Warm Heart, Pooch & Bobo and Uh Oh!

Patagonia Outlet Store
36 West Santa Clara Street
Ventura, CA 93001
(see Freeport, ME for merchandise discription)
(805) 648-3803

Payment: All major credit cards and checks
Phone orders accepted

Patagonia Outlet Store
3267 Highland Drive
Salt Lake City, UT 84106
(801) 466-2226

Patagonia Outlet
34 North Idaho
Dillon, MT 59725
(406) 683-2580

Trumpette Factory Store
108 Kentucky
Petaluma, CA 94952
(707) 769-1173

Even kids' clothes manufacturers march to the beat of a different drummer when they emanate out of Los Angeles—case in point, Trumpette kid clothes. Remember the Dairy council ad for milk, "Got Milk?" That commercial was outfitted by Trumpette. If that's not wacky enough for you, how about a romper that looks like a Campbell's soup can? If that's a little too much for you, Trumpette does a simpler design spelling out either "boy" or "girl" across the front of a pink or blue garment. Yes, they have basics here, too (great fabrics), including corduroy pants, leggings, sweat coordinates and thermal tops for boys and girls size 3 months to 8 years. Prices at the factory store are a little above wholesale—figure around 40% of retail. They will take your order over the phone and ship anywhere.

Petals Outlet Store
250 Great Mall Drive
Milpitas, CA 95035
(408) 934-9717

Hours: Mon.–Fri 10–9; Sat 10–8; Sun. 10–7
Payment: Visa, MC and checks

I don't mean to be a "Petal" pusher, but you really must get over to this outlet store. I fell in love with these dresses when I first spotted them in the children's trade magazines. Petals uses only the best fabrics and full European styling. You'll find sizes 12 months–14 years in dresses and playwear. After the retail stores have received their shipments, the outlet store gets the leftovers and sells them at 50% reductions. **News flash!** Petals has just launched a dancewear line called Sweet Tarts. If your child is involved in dance, skating, acrobatics or gymnastics, you know how expensive athletic togs can be. This outlet is now selling leotards, unitards, dance skirts, crop tops, bike shorts and knitted sweats for under $15 (for example, bike shorts are $5.99). Everything is final sale.

Sara's Prints Outlet Store
3018 A Alvarado Street
San Leandro, CA 94577
(510) 352-6060

Hours: Mon.–Fri. 10–4
Payment: Visa, MC and checks

Normally, you can't utter the words "100% cotton pajamas" in the same breath without raising a safety ruckus; however, Sara's Prints has it all figured out. They do make—gasp—100% cotton pajamas; however, they are made from a specially treated, flame-retardant cotton. At the outlet store you'll find closeouts, past-season goods and seconds at 30%–50% off regular retail prices. The company specializes in layette, pajamas, nightgowns and long underwear in attractive and playful prints. All sizes can be found here from infant through preteen 16.

Storybook Heirlooms Outlet
8300 Arroyo A-60
Gilroy, CA 95020
(408) 842-3880

Phone orders accepted
Free catalog

7400 South Las Vegas Blvd. #47
Las Vegas, NV 89123
(702) 896-4663

As we mentioned earlier in the book, save those catalogs. Here's why. If you're familiar with Storybook Heirlooms, then you already know about this dreamy catalog of exquisite children's special-occasion and better casual wear. You also know about the hefty prices attached to everything in the catalog. Well, weep no more, for discounts of 40% off catalog prices (current and past-season merchandise), you can visit the stores or place an order over the phone. Call (800) 825-6565 to receive catalogs on a regular basis. Remember to hang onto all catalogs for future ordering purposes. The stores stock overruns, samples and some seconds. In the past the catalog has featured some of the most renowned labels in childrens-wear such as Sylvia Whyte, Sarah Kent, Mousefeathers and Amiana shoes. However, you should know that Storybook is phasing out many of these lines in favor of their own "Storybook Heirlooms" line, which includes casual wear, special-occasion dressing and mother/daughter looks. Expect even bigger reductions at the end of seasons; for example, after Christmas they take an additional 50% off! Enjoy; this is one of our favorite finds.

Sweet Potatoes Outlet Store
1716 Fourth Street
Berkeley, CA 94710
(510) 527-7633

Hours: Mon.–Sat. 10–6; Sun. 11–6
Payment: Visa, MC, Discover, checks

Harvest the savings at the outlet store that offers Sweet Potatoes, Spuds, New Potatoes, Marimekko and Yazoo at 30%–60% off retail prices. Seen in the more expensive children's catalogs, these higher-ticket sportswear collections are beautifully designed and very child-flattering. You'll find samples and current merch andise in most sizes starting from 3 months and up to size 12. Mailing list provided for extra sale notices. Get busy and get on it.

We Be Bop Factory Store
1380 10th Street
Berkeley, CA 94710
(510) 527-7256

Hours: Mon.–Fri. 10–5; Sat. 10–6; Sun. 12–5
Payment: Visa, AmEx, checks

We be happy about the prices on these very hip looking clothes for groovy kids! Expect to pay 25%–50% off regular retail here. Originally created as a sophisticated preteen line for kids' sizes 7–14, they've added an infant through toddler line. Baby designs feature over-dyed cotton bubbles, rompers and jump suits. The preteen line highlights filtered-down junior looks in rayon and cotton. You'll find lots of floral granny dresses, full-styled pants, cropped jackets, blazers and some accessories, including footwear.

Wee Clancy Warehouse/ Outlet Store
2682 Middlefield Road
Redwood City, CA 94063
(415) 366-5597

Hours: Thurs. and Fri. 10–4; Sat 9–1
Payment: Call store for information

This company was more than a wee bit paranoid about getting

mentioned in this book. Translation: great bargains for you! Wee Clancy manufactures better girls' dresses found in upscale department stores and specialty boutiques. Their outlet store, which is actually part of the warehouse, sells off size 6 months to size 16 dresses at 50% off retail prices. Call the above number and place yourself on the mailing list for upcoming sale event notices. (If there's no one available to take your call, a recorded message will inform you of upcoming sale events and kickoff sales, and will also take your name and address for inclusion on the mailing list.)

Midwest Region

Bercot Childrenswear Outlet
1915 South Calhoun Street
Fort Wayne, IN 46802
(219) 456-9739

Hours: Mon.–Fri. 10–5
Payment: AmEx, MC, Visa, Discover, checks

Here's another true factory store set up right in front of the factory. It's so close, in fact, that you can hear the sewing machines humming! Get on the mailing list for their super clearance sales and you'll save up to 75% off retail prices! This fashion line of boys' and girls' coordinated cotton separates is available in sizes 6 months to 7 years. They carry first-quality overruns at 20%–50% off retail.

Boo! Warehouse Store
18 North 4th Street
Suite 506
Minneapolis, MN 55401
(612) 376-0585

Hours: Mon.–Fri. 9–5
Payment: MC, Visa, checks
Catalog and phone orders accepted

Don't let Boo! scare you; their prices are good. Take this opportunity to call for the Boo! catalog of non-traditional, polar fleece outerwear, vintage farm dressing, retro dresses, skirts, pants, moccasins, cozy baby blankets and bunting at wholesale and below prices! This is a very high-end line of children's clothes seen in upscale fashion magazines. We're especially fond of their trademark, buffalo-check winter jacket with fringe detail, and the nostalgic collection of picnic-check dresses with apron overlay. The boys' line is equally unique, featuring old-time farmer overalls. Take an additional 10%–20% off during their back-to-school and Christmas sales. Call to get on the mailing list for postcard notices.

Cottontail Originals Retail Factory Store
720 South Main
Stillwater, OK 74074
(405) 624-9360

Hours: Mon.–Wed. 10–6; Thurs 10–8; Fri. 10–6; Sat. 10–5:30
Payment: Visa, AmEx, Discover
Phone orders accepted

With the factory for Cottontails just a hop, skip and a jump across town, you can save around 30% off retail or better, by visiting or phone-ordering from their outlet store for traditional, but contemporary, kid clothes for boys and girls. If you love the way kids look in linen dresses and separates, and you know how difficult they are to find, you'll be happy to know that Cottontails loves the way kids look in linen, too! Cottontails specializes in 100% cotton separates, dresses, short sets, onesies, rompers, suspender sets and mother/daughter looks. Rayon seems to be making its way into the line now, too. Lots of beautiful prints from gingham checks to daisies.

Echo Field Factory Store
3304 West 44th Street
Minneapolis, MN 55408
(612) 474-5032

Hours: Mon.–Fri. 9–8; Sat. 10–5; Sun. 12–4

Payment: MC, Visa, checks
Phone orders accepted

17770 Highway 7
Minnetonka, MN 55345

Truly outstanding in their "field," these huge stores offer spring/summer and fall/winter goods all year round from 40%–70% off retail prices. Echo Field is known for their charming, 100% cotton (high-quality and very durable) playwear in child-flattering styles. Lots of dresses and matching leggings, bubbles for baby, tank tops, capri sets, one-piece zipper rompers that facilitate diaper changing and their beautiful, double-sided receiving blankets with dual-sided prints.

Florence Eiseman Outlet Stores
425 Lighthouse Place
Michigan City, IN 46360
(219) 879-1767

Hours: Mon.–Sat. 9–8; Sun. 9–6
Payment: MC, Visa
Phone orders accepted
(also see Lancaster, PA)

Once again, a Midwestern opportunity to purchase the classic Eiseman collection for boys size infant–7 and girls size infant–14, at 30% off and more. Merchandise here runs a year behind; however, a classic is a classic. Phone orders available if you can't get to the store. We love everything, but you've got to try their bathing suits—simply scrumptious fabrics and delightful designs.

Heart's Outlet Store
11650 West 85th Street
Lenexa, KS 66214
(913) 492-6078

Hours: Mon.–Fri. 8–4:30; Sat. 10–4
Payment: Visa, MC, Discover and checks
Phone orders accepted

Learn this one by "heart," because they'll send you beautiful children's clothes at 25%–60% off the retail department store prices. This factory-direct store is so helpful that folks around the country let them pick and choose their kids' wardrobe sight-unseen. Pretty girl's' dresses called "Heartbeats" are available here for $20–$50 (prices drop even further during their twice-a-year blow-out sale in January and July). Heart's is known for their appliquéd casualwear, brother/sister looks, fleece sets, overalls, shorts and jams, t-shirts, denim and coordinating hair accessories, hats and socks. They also do a big mother/daughter business, coordinating mom's jumper to daughter's dresses. Sizes start at 6 months and go up to size 12 for both boys and girls.

Oilily Factory Store
Lighthouse Place
Michigan City, IN 46360
(219) 872-3577

Hours: Vary; call for exact schedule
Catalog and phone orders accepted

2700 Potomac Mills Circle
Prince William, VA 22192
(703) 491-2926

Hours: Mon.–Fri. 10–9:30; Sat. and Sun. 10–6:30
Payment: Visa, MC, AmEx, checks

These are the only outlet stores for this very pricey line of whimsical kid clothes from Holland. Call (800) 977-7736 to order catalogs and remember to save them! The store will ship past-season goods (we've found their "past-season" to be "in-season" for us) to you at 35%–50% off retail prices depending on the time of year. Merchandise is 35% off everyday with additional reductions of 10%–20% taken during their Thanksgiving weekend sale, after Christmas and at the end of the summer season. Call the Indiana store to be placed on the mailing list so that you can take advantage of these great sales. Store hours vary throughout the year; call for exact schedule.

Rachel T
Factory Store
1500 Iron Street
North Kansas City, MO 64116
(816) 472-6056

Hours: Mon.–Fri. 7–3:30
Payment: Checks and cash only

(Would the boy's line be Mr. T?) These full-fashioned European-styled dresses for girls sizes 12 months to 12 years are available here at 50% below retail prices. From buffalo check to plaid taffeta, corduroy, cotton prints and velvets with or without lace trim, you'll find an enormous selection of lovely frocks from $21–$60!

Treasures of Annie's Antics
Factory Store
2045 West Maple Road East
Walled Lake, MI 48390
(810) 669-6010

Hours: Mon.–Fri. 9–5
Payment: Checks, cash

This genuine factory store (the manufacturing plant is connected to the outlet by a series of doors) offers artisan-quality, hand-knit and crocheted sweaters, vests and cardigans. Annie's Antics takes special care in yarn selection and even goes so far as to roll and combine their own yarn for unique results. Antique and vintage buttons finish off their designs to create a very special look. Prices at the store are a little above wholesale, which generally means around 30%–40% off retail. You'll also find Flapdoodles here at discount prices.

Sample Sales

In order to be on the cutting edge of fashion without cutting into your budget, you'll most certainly want to check out sample sales where the very latest styles are available at the very lowest prices. Some of the more fabulous items in my daughter's closet came from sample sales. As an added bonus, samples are usually in tip top condition; after all, these are the actual garments presented to buyers for the purpose of selling to major department stores and specialty boutiques, so they better look good.

The sample sales, for the most part, take place at showrooms within major city fashion marts or children's design buildings. So keep in mind that you'll be entering a "trade" building that is neither designed nor set up for selling merchandise to the general public. In fact, many showroom leases have a clause that reads, "no showroom sample sales allowed." Thankfully, this clause is largely ignored. However, discretion is the better part of valor here; in other words, try to blend in. We urge you to dress and behave in a quiet, business-like manner. Be observant; if you see buyers at the tables, do not scream out, "hey, where are the samples?" Softly and politely inquire as to where the samples racks are and go about your business quickly and unobtrusively. The rep may even ask you to come back after the buyers have left. Do not be offended; although they are making some quick cash from you, their main business is sitting at the table and they don't want to jeopardize that.

Once inside the showroom, you'll find that these manufacturer and designer representatives are selling off salesmen samples and sometimes actual stock merchandise that wasn't sold to buyers (left-overs), canceled orders or returned goods. These sales can take place at any time depending on what they have in the showroom. You're more likely to find the largest selection of goods at the end of their selling season, which usually means the next season for you. For example, sample sales taking place in January and February consist of goods from the end of the spring selling season, which hasn't arrived yet! (There may also be fall/winter merchandise mixed in at way below wholesale prices.)

We suggest that you get your name on all showroom mailing lists for notification of exact dates and times of sample sales throughout the year. It's also a good idea to keep in touch with the reps by phone as they don't always get around to sending out the advance sale notice cards, or they may decide at the last minute to hold a sale. If you happen to be in the area of these trade buildings, you can often just run up to the showroom floors and look for "sample sale" signs posted on the doors. The following is a list of showrooms and reps that have been holding sample sales on a fairly regular basis over the past few years. A final word: Bring cash and leave the kids home.

Sample Sales New York City

Creation Stummer
131 W. 33rd Street
Room 819
New York City, NY 10001
(212) 695-8770

Payment: Cash only

This tastefully executed and very expensive line of better children's sportswear, rompers, jackets, dresses and skirts becomes very affordable at their twice-a-year sample and stock sales. Expect to wait in line, which means crowded conditions inside the showroom. We've seen some other clothing lines at these events that you might also be interested in such as Delaware, Jet Club and Boboli. Lots of sizes and lots of merchandise. Call for sale dates and bring cash. Once again, no children! Sales usually take place around the end of October and sometime in April.

Curly Girls Sample Sale
112 West 34th Street
Suite 414
New York City, NY 10120
(212) 967-6457

One of the better showrooms in the children's design buildings, they represent such "in-fashion" manufacturers as MAC, Jumpers, Viaggi, Monsterwear, EIEIO and Simi dresses. Sales here are on again and off again. But if you give them a call you can be pretty sure that a sample sale isn't far off. Do ask about sizes because the selection varies from sale to sale. Expect to pay around wholesale prices for boy's and girl's merchandise.

Guess & Baby Guess Sample Sale
112 West 34th Street
Room 807
New York City, NY 10120
(212) 629-8760

Payment: Cash only

Can you guess how low the prices are here? You guessed it! Find a large assortment of styles and sizes here at 50% below retail and sometimes lower. Only one problem here: The samples don't always have clearly marked sizes. But you know what to do. Just bring some items from your kid's closet and compare length and width. There, you sized it yourself! Call for sale dates.

Identity Sample Sale
1466 Broadway (42nd Street)
Suite 900
New York City, NY 10036
(212) 719-1026

Payment: Cash only

If you love those expensive leather and wool baseball jackets sold at trendy boutiques and 1950s-style soda shops, then you don't want to miss this!. We've visited the Identity showroom throughout the winter months to check on the kids inventory and were thrilled to find these attractive jackets at 50% off retail prices! Size availability was a little jumpy with a few smalls and some big kid sizes, 7–12 years. The pink and white, embroidered stadium jacket for little girls is our all-time favorite. **Bargain Bonus:** adult sizes available too. Call first to make sure they have what you're looking for.

Jack Morris Sample Sale
112 West 34th Street
Room 1618
New York City, NY 10120
(212) 239-8232

Payment: Cash and checks with identification

This was my first sample sale and oh what a feeling! There was a respectably sized line outside the door waiting for the showroom to open. "They must know something," I thought. They did. This was one of the larger sample sales in the building, I was told. The selection of sizes was impressive, but the labels inside the clothes were even more impressive. This was one of those sales that makes you want to kick yourself. The beautiful Robin International coat and hat I had just purchased at retail for $140 (remember, this was before my "bargain enlightenment") was there for $75. Mouse-feathers dresses in assorted sizes were in abundance at 50% off retail prices—their "paper doll" collection was precious. Other lines spotted at these sample and stock sales through the years include Plum Pudding, Ali Mac polar fleece novelty coats, Une Deux Trois, Zoodles, Lili Wang, Vive La Fete and more. I've received some advance-notice cards from them in the past; however, they can't be counted on. You're better off calling to find out when the next sale is.

Jacksen Associates Sample Sale

131 W. 33rd Street
Suite 1101
New York City, NY 10001
(212) 564-5168

Payment: Cash only

A stocking stuffer's delight, you may want to put this one on your holiday gift list. If you're familiar with those fancy, overpriced, personalized gift stores featuring everything from coat racks to picture frames to bulletin boards, that's the type of merchandise you'll find at this showroom, only for about half price. Jacksen Associates traditionally holds sales right before Christmas; however, they may let you up during the year if you need something in particular. It's a good idea to call and see if they have what you want. Remember to stock up on gifts and don't overlook the party favors.

Jean Bourget Sample and Stock Sale

112 West 34th Street
Room 612
New York City, NY 10020
(212) 279-7672

Moms in the fashion know are familiar with this timeless and beautifully designed line of French sportswear and outer-wear for boys and girls. We recommend planning ahead and buying larger sizes at these great prices. Jean Bourget never goes out of style. Extra-long hems give you the ability to cuff and roll down as the child grows. We kept our daughter in the same pair of Bourget pants for three years! (We occasionally threw them both in the wash.) In tracking these sales over the years, the pattern seems to be November, March or April sales. Keep in touch with them and they'll let you know when the next event will be held.

Kourageous Kids

131 West 33rd Street
Suite 312
New York City, NY 10001
(212) 244-0431

One of the more avant-garde showrooms, I've picked up some terrific patched Trouble jeans and matching T-shirts, retro palazzo pants, rayon tops and lots of accessories at below wholesale prices. You'll have to call to find out when these sporadic sample and stock sales take place, but it's well worth the small effort of a phone call for savings this big and beautiful! Other lines found here include Lili Wang (crisis-cross straps and full skirts with crinolines), Radical Rags and Flowers by Zoe. Sizes may be limited, so ask what's in stock before visiting the showroom.

Polo Norte Furs Sample Sale

463 Seventh Avenue at 35th Street
New York City, NY 10018
(212) 594-4475

Payment: Visa, MC
Phone orders accepted
No returns

You can call this showroom to find out what stock is available and when is the best time to shop. Beautifully styled, long-haired and sheared rabbit jackets, parkas and coats are offered at wholesale and below prices. In the past there have been stunning, unisex shearlings with toggle closures in black, antique brown and cognac. Many rabbit and shearling coats have hoods, some detachable. A variety of colors and trims (i.e. Mongolian lamb) are here in sizes toddler through 14. Some adult coats, too, at incredibly low prices. Prices start at $70 and go up to $200.

Rachel's Trousseau Sample and Stock Sales
112 West 34th Street
Suite 1606
New York City, NY 10120
(212) 695-2512

Payment: Cash only

Splendid European fashions for boys and girls are available throughout the year. You'll find all seasons and across-the-board styles, including very upscale dresses, coats, bathing suits, shorts and t-shirts. In the past we've seen Pito, Pito and exquisite Cachelle special-occasion dresses. Call for dates and bring cash.

Richard Kutner Sample Sale
131 W. 33rd Street
Suite 801
New York City, NY 10001
(212) 594-3740

Payment: Cash only

Top-of-the-line imports seen at upscale boutiques around the country are offered here for one week every November at 30% below wholesale prices! They generally have a little bit of everything, including bathing suits, dresses, skirts, winter coats and more. This showroom reps Clayeux, Miniman of France, David Charles of England and Newman. This is one tremendous sample and stock sale featuring most sizes from infant through preteen. They do have a mailing list that will alert you to the exact date and time of sale. A word of caution: They are very strict about time. Get there one minute too late and you're out of luck and out of goodies for your kids! Absolutely no kids or strollers.

Pamela Company Sample & Stock Sale
150 W. 28th Street
Room #1004
New York City, NY 10001
(212) 255-8233

Payment: Cash only

Get a jump on next Halloween and stock your child's costume trunk, or wardrobe the next recital or class play at this annual sample sale held in December. This multi-talented designer offers her exquisite tutus, be-ribboned fantasy skirts, whimsical wands, headbands, head-pieces and much more at wholesale prices. We've seen some creative kids pair up her tulle-net crinolines with jean jackets, leggings and Converse hi-top sneakers for a great, funky look—something a little different to wear out to dinner or to a party! Call at the end of November for sale dates. **Bargain Bonus:** Adult sizes here too!

The Rose Garden
112 West 34th Street
Room 416
New York City, NY 10120
(212) 564-5100

Payment: Cash only

Awesome savings are continually blooming at this showroom of high-ticket lines seen in such toney department stores as Bloomingdales. In fact, during the holiday season, I visited Bloomies kid's department and found some of the exact same

Monkeywear items at The Rose Garden showroom at half the regular retail price. Now, they don't have all sizes, but it's certainly worth a phone call or visit. Other fashion-forward manufacturers represented at the Rose Garden include Bisou, Bisou, Awesome Graphics, Marsha Inc., Y Not, Cache, Cache, Sarah Kent and more. Samples seem to available on a continual basis. Call first to determine the best time to visit the showroom.

Rudin Needlecraft Sample Sale
112 West 34th Street
Suite 609
New York City, NY 10120
(212) 947-8316

Payment: Cash only

Gotta baby? Need a baby gift? You may want to try this showroom, which specializes in fine-knit layette, infant sweaters, shawls, caps and blankets. Sporadic sample sales will allow you the opportunity to purchase these darling outfits found in better department stores at wholesale and below prices. They may be limited in sizes to 6 and 12 months, so inquire about size availability before you go up. No mailing list here, so you'll need to call to find out when it's best to visit. (If they're not too busy, they'll be happy to help showroom passers-by.)

Seibel & Stern Sample Sale
112 West 34th Street
Suite 1100
New York City, NY 10120
(212) 563-0326

Payment: Cash only

Terrific bargains are often available here throughout the year. They will occasionally send out sale notices; however, you'd be wiser to call them about sale times. You will find moderately priced girls' dresses (Kim and Little Star) in most sizes. We've also seen some boys and girls sportswear separates (for example, sweats) here at times. Prices range from $2 and go up to around $20. Bring cash.

Wippette Sample Sale
500 Seventh Avenue
14th Floor
New York City, NY 10019
(212) 852-4900

Payment: Cash only

No, not a tribute to the classic Devo song, but a good, "Wippette good," raincoat sale, anyway. This one usually takes place annually in December. For the cost-conscious parent reluctant to spend big bucks on rainwear, you'll be delighted to discover that your bank account won't get washed out with these low prices! You can pick up a stylish, brightly colored, vinyl raincoat with hood for under $10. Once again, take advantage of this terrific sale opportunity and buy gifts for future use at these unbeatable prices. Bring cash and call them for the next sale date.

Sample Sales Boston

Bayside Merchandise Mart
150–160 Mt. Vernon St.
Boston, MA 02125
(617) 474-6518

Payment: Cash only

This merchandise mart operates in a similar fashion to the children's design buildings in New York—sample sale signs are placed on showroom doors. However, security may be a little tighter here so it might not be a bad idea to call the mart and order the childrenswear directory first. You can then call showrooms before you go, determine if they have samples and then forewarn them that you're coming and they can put your name on a guest list—just in case the guard asks you where you're going. Children's showrooms can be found on the first and second floors. Even if there isn't a sample sign on the door, if you notice the showroom isn't crowded, it's perfectly alright to ask if there are any samples for sale.

Sample Sales West Coast

Calif3ornia Mart
110 East Ninth Street
Los Angeles, CA 90079-2827
(800) CAL-MART

Payment: Cash

This mart opens its doors to anxious parents ready to score great bargains on the last Friday of every month. Simply head up to the sixth floor of the mart and follow the crowds, or look for "samples for salc" signs dis played on showroom doors. You can call the mart and order a directory listing the room numbers and clothing lines carried by all reps in the building. There may be a nominal charge for the guide.

The Sample Room Sample Sales
699 8th Street
Suite 6206
San Francisco, CA 94103
(415) 621-9945

Hours: Mon.–Fri. 8:30–5
Payment: Cash only

This one is right in the Fashion Mart, so you'll need to call first and make an appointment in order to have your name placed on the building's guest list. You'll find a full range of sizes—boys: infant–7, girls: infant–14—in snowsuits, pram suits, parkas, windbreakers, polar fleece outerwear, ski bibs, swimsuits, jogging sets, sportswear, dresses, denim coordinates, tights, socks, accessories and more at wholesale and below prices. Moderate to upscale brands are featured all year long.

San Francisco Fashion Center
Exhibit Hall
699 8th Street
San Francisco, CA 94103
(800) STYLE-SF

Payment: Check or cash

Converge on the group sample sales for men, women and kids held four times a year at Exhibit Hall, and save up to 50%–75% off list prices on very hip designer collections and better brands. Dates for the sales are set each December for the following year. So get yourself on the mailing list by calling the above phone number.
The 95,000-square-foot Exhibit Hall hosts approximately 15–20 children's reps offering trendy bargains in size infant through 16. There is a $3 admission fee for adults, but kids under 12 are free. By placing your name on the mailing list you will receive a discount coupon good toward the price of admission. These quarterly sample sales are also advertised in local papers such as the *San Francisco Chronicle*. Available facilities include a catered food service, coffee shop and numerous rest rooms.

Midwestern Sample Sales

Chicago Apparel Center
350 North Orleans Street
Chicago, IL 60654
(312) 527-7777

Payment: Cash only

Feel free to browse the sixth floor of the Chicago Apparel Center for children's samples from well-known manufacturers. Some showrooms will display "samples for sale" notices on the doors. You might want to call the above phone number and order a market guide first. Then, call up the various reps handling the lines you're interested in and inquire about their sample sales. Don't forget to ask about size availability. Here are a few showrooms and reps that have had wonderful samples and prices through the years.

Nat Fantl
Room 612
(312) 467-5325

This showroom has samples most of the time. You'll find bathing suits, shorts sets, dresses, sweatsuits and assorted sports wear. They carry moderate to better labels such as Jessica McClintock, Bullfrog, Le Top, Peaches & Cream, Petals dresses and much more. Prices should be around wholesale or less.

Judi Kadden
Suite 6-110
(312) 644-1763

Great samples and top-notch lines are available sporadically at wholesale prices. Impressive collections spotted here have included Hot Tot, Golden Rainbow, Maxou, Rubbies, Sara, Sara, Baby Lulu, Agabang, Mulberibush, and other very trendy kid clothes.

Robert Kaul
Room 6-113
(312) 527-1662

Select sizes in better childrens wear is continually proffered here at wholesale prices. If you love the tailored look of Monkeywear blazers, skirts and pants, then stop by and pick up a great buy! Find oodles of Zoodles, Sweet Potatoes, Nautica, Plum Pudding, Jumpers and Cary too.

CHAPTER TWO

SUITE DREAMS: FABULOUS AND FRUGAL FURNITURE FINDS

When I began my search for nursery necessities, I was clueless and under the impression that the only place to shop for top-quality designer-type juvenile furniture and bedding were pricey specialty shops like Bellini. It simply never occurred to me that you could find a good selection of upscale brand furniture in an assortment of styles at deeply discounted prices with superior service thrown in as a bonus.

Ten years of research later, I am still kicking myself over the wasted dollars I could have invested in a nice zero coupon bond for my daughter's college education! Fortunately, you'll profit from my mistakes by finding that top-of-the-line children's furniture, fabric, wallpapers, and bedding are all available at off-price showrooms, galleries, outlets, and warehouses, or via mail order—at discounts ranging from 25% to 70% off list price. Once you know where to go, or who to call, you have no reason to shop for these items at elite boutiques and upscale department stores.

Specialty boutiques strive to maintain a precious image by convincing customers that their merchandise cannot be purchased cheaper anywhere else, adding to the "exclusive" image of these products. Don't believe this propaganda. *The Smart Shopper's Guide* has tracked down the best furniture bargains for kids and will take you directly to the sources where you can find almost anything at significant discounts.

Creating an adorable and unique dream-room for your baby, toddler, child, or preteen does not have to cost you a small fortune or take lots of time. You can do much of the legwork by ordering directly from your home. In fact, many of the companies listed in this chapter can send you catalogs, swatches, and window treatment samples.

Savvy Shopping Strategies and Consumer Caveats

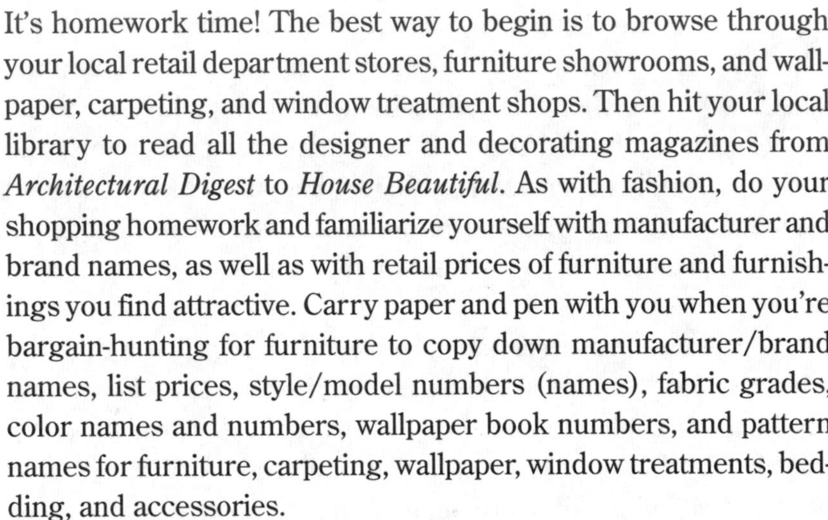

It's homework time! The best way to begin is to browse through your local retail department stores, furniture showrooms, and wallpaper, carpeting, and window treatment shops. Then hit your local library to read all the designer and decorating magazines from *Architectural Digest* to *House Beautiful*. As with fashion, do your shopping homework and familiarize yourself with manufacturer and brand names, as well as with retail prices of furniture and furnishings you find attractive. Carry paper and pen with you when you're bargain-hunting for furniture to copy down manufacturer/brand names, list prices, style/model numbers (names), fabric grades, color names and numbers, wallpaper book numbers, and pattern names for furniture, carpeting, wallpaper, window treatments, bedding, and accessories.

Bargain Byte

Leading department stores may have their own numbering system, so it's better to get manufacturer names, style numbers, and group names from local furniture stores. Manufacturer names may be stamped inside panels of the furniture. Department store sales people may let you look at the manufacturer brochures that list style numbers or names. You may find these brochures in drawers. The salesperson may even let you take home the brochure. If you need to write down the information, try to be discreet.

Even among the discounters and off-price merchants, prices often vary so you still need to comparison-shop. When you're calling the various discount sources cited in this book, keep a log of the price quotes for each item so you can easily see which prices are the lowest.

To achieve a decorator look without going to the expense of hiring one, simply do what the decorators do. Put together your own *samples baggy*. All you need is one of those plastic Ziploc bags into which you place selected carpet swatches, fabric remnants, paint chips, blind or window treatment samples, wallpaper bits, and room/window measurements. (You can even purchase a small piece of oaktag and sketch a master plan, complete with dimensions and measurements, to which you can attach all samples and swatches in the appropriate areas.) If you are decorating several rooms, you may want to purchase a small photo album and assign one room per page. This is precisely how top designers work.

Why a samples baggy? Let's say you haven't picked out carpeting yet, but you have decided on the wallpaper for the room. Don't make the mistake of thinking you can match the carpet color to a color within the wallpaper by memory alone! Do you know how many shades of beige exist in the world? Some shades have brown tones, some have green tones, and some have yellow tones . . . you get the picture. You must have a piece of the wallpaper to hold up next to the carpet swatch for color comparison purposes. (You may want to make your samples baggy a permanent part of your pocketbook, tote, or backpack. You never know when you may come across that something extra for the room that needs to be color coordinated or measured for an exact fit!)

Here are some insider secrets from furniture experts:

- For that opulent pillow look, buy oversized pillows to fit inside pillowcases and shams. Pillows are so malleable that you can easily squeeze them into a case that is one size smaller. For example, if you have a standard size pillow sham, try inserting a queen-size pillow rather than the standard size. The increased fullness lends a true professional decorator touch and makes for a beautiful look.
- If your child loves to jump on the bed, consider an upholstered headboard. The first time I discovered feelings for my younger sister Lori (she was three and I was seven) was the day she jumped on the bed and fell onto a wooden headboard—teeth first. I will spare you the grisly details, but needless to say, my daughter has an upholstered headboard. Apart from the safety aspect, upholstered headboards are elegant and generally cheaper than formica and wooden beds. You can choose your own fabric from a local fabric outlet store (ask about fabric closeouts for real bargains), then decide on

the shape of the headboard and finishing trim. Comparison-shop through your phone book and local newspapers for upholsterers (fabric outlet stores may have additional leads for you). You may want to purchase extra fabric to make a matching quilt, pillowcase shams, window treatments, even coordinating doll clothes to complete the ensemble look.

- High-priced furniture does not automatically mean high-quality furniture. Don't assume that the costly cribs, changing tables, dressers, and youth beds in fancy imported juvenile furniture boutiques are always worth the overinflated hangtag prices. Pull a drawer out of their "museum-quality" dresser and examine the goods up close and personal. Ask the salesperson about joinery—how the sides of the drawer are held together. You want either dovetailed joints (interlocking wooden extensions that hold the sides of drawers together) or mortise-and-tenon joints (a large peg that fits securely into the same-shaped opening). You don't want sides of the drawer that are set up next to each other at a right angle and held together by glue, nails, or staples. After I spent way too much money on a dresser from one of those exclusive baby emporiums, I found that if I put a few too many baby clothes in a drawer, that drawer would pull away, exposing sharp, unraveled staples. The store's unsatisfactory solution was to shoot in extra staples! Become an informed consumer and learn what constitutes well-made quality furniture. Buying a good piece of furniture at greatly reduced prices is just as easy, and more rewarding, than buying good furniture at overinflated retail prices.

- You can upgrade cribs, strollers, high chairs, and blinds with new hardware, harnesses, and fabric seats by calling manufacturer customer service lines for needed parts. (Try calling the 1-800 phone directory first for phone numbers.) Updating items yourself is much more economical than buying everything new! It's always a good idea to keep in touch with manufacturers of your major nursery and juvenile pieces anyway so you're notified of recalls or parts replacement information.

- Decorate with an eye toward the future. Think twice about wallpapering with those cutesy, juvenile prints or theme motifs that your kids will quickly outgrow. Leave these wallpapers to the pediatrician's office where they belong. Pastels, muted pastels, floral prints, or primary geometrics work well in a baby's room and are sophisticated enough to satisfy the most arrogant adolescent. If you can't resist the urge to babify the nursery or child's room, use a juvenile-type border rather than floor-to-ceiling wallpaper. The border is much easier and cheaper to remove than a room full of wallpaper. You can decorate the rest of the walls inexpensively with the latest trend in high-style decorator kids' rooms—sponge painting, marbleizing, ragging-rolling, stippling, or combing. Supplies, do-it-yourself instructions, sample classes, or video demonstrations are available at paint stores such as Janovic Plaza or Color Age and home center retailers such as Pergament, Home Depot, etc. You would be amazed at what a natural sea sponge can do for your walls! The results are stunning, and of course, the best part is that you don't need to remove expensive wallpaper when you or your kid is tired of it. You just paint right over it.

- Avoid fantasy theme decorating with racecar and spaceship beds. Designers call this technique a "time-lock." Not only is your kid likely to tire of these theme beds, but many of them are poorly constructed. My dear friend Dorothy thought that nothing would make her son happier than sleeping in a race car. She went out and purchased the flashiest Corvette car bed imaginable, complete with steering wheel. Little Alex loved his bed, but when it came time to read bedtime stories, ouch! There was no place for mom to sit comfortably. The sides of the car rose way up over the mattress, preventing anyone from sitting side-straddle on the bed. Now, mom has to perform gymnastics to find a space in this cramped little car bed. This problem brings up another obstacle with these beds: how do you make a bed with such high sides? The answer: with much difficulty.

- It's all in the finishing, according to top interior designers and magazine editors. Accessories can make or break the look of a room. In a child's room, try to carry through the dominant color story right down to the toys, doll clothes, lamps, book covers, and even pet cages! Yes, bird cages, gerbil environments, and fish tanks come in designer colors today. There's no excuse for putting a black metal-rimmed aquarium in a little girl's cotton-candy-pink and white room. If I could find a pink bird cage, so can you! (You don't have to find a pink bird. However, it can't hurt to look for one that blends in. After all, birds *are* decorative—and they also sing our favorite song: cheep!)

Where The Buys Are

This section provides the names, addresses, and ordering information for the best discount furniture sources.

Southeast

Alman's Home Furnishings

110 East First St.
Newton, NC 28658
(800) 729-0422
(704) 464-3204

Hours: 8:30–5:30 daily except Wed.

Payment: Visa, MC, AmEx
Publications available: store mailer and catalogs

The very helpful staff here was familiar with the stock and quick to point out comparable collections at lower price points. For example, after I mentioned the Thomasville Ribbons & Bows group, my salesperson said that I could get the same look for much less in the Vaughan-Bassett line and that she would immediately send me photocopies of these pieces. Other lines available here are Stanley, Lexington, Bassett (including cribs), and Broyhill. Expect to pay around 35% off list price, including shipping, for children's items.

Check out Lexington's spectacular new Art Cetera line, the most detailed and heavily embellished of the new handpainted look. Look through the catalog to see myriad designs including a rainforest theme on white or dark green headboards, trunks with stars and geometrics, forest friends chest, zookeeper's cabinet, sun, moon and stars bookcase, and much more. Lexington even donates a portion of profits to the children's charity CARE through its Kids Care program.

Alman's also can assist you in purchasing cribs and youth groups from Bassett, Simmons, Stanley, and Vaughan-Bassett. For those partial to the decorative appliqué look, you may want to take a look at Vaughan-Bassett's Farmhouse Collection in washed pine and Shaker styling. Figure on 40% to 50% off retail prices here.

America's Finest Furniture
Discounter Referral Service
(910) 884-0163

Hours: Mon.–Sat. 10–6

If you know the manufacturer you're interested in but are having difficulty finding a discount outlet, this service represents a number of furniture clients who may be able to help you. There's no charge for the referral service; you pay only for your phone call.

Barnes & Barnes
190 Commerce Ave.
Yadkin Park
Southern Pines, NC 28387
(800) 334-8174

Hours: Mon.–Fri. 9–5
Payment: Visa, MC
Publications available: brochure and mailer

Barnes & Barnes sells the regular kids' lines of Lexington, Bassett (yes, cribs), Stanley, and Lea, along with Crawford (more traditional looks in maple wood) and Lynn Hollyn for teenage girls. In addition, the outlet represents some of the finest fabric houses such as Schumacher, Waverly, Kravet, Robert Allen, Mitchell, Payne, and AMSCO. The store is small; the bulk of business is via phone and mail. Expect to pay slightly over wholesale prices or about 40% off retail.

Better Homes Furniture Outlet
P.O. Box 1016
248 1st Avenue, NW
Hickory, NC 28601
(704) 328-8302

Hours: Mon., Tues., Thurs., Fri. 8:30–5; Sat 8:30–3
Payment: Cash and checks only
Publications available: store mailer

Some of the very lowest prices in North Carolina are here, and you can count on 50% off suggested retail prices, possibly a little more. We also can't say enough about the staff; they were informative, patient, and delightfully friendly. Have a look at the Shaw Furniture Gallery listing for my shopper's comparison test. Better Homes passed our Lexington Betsy Cameron Children's Collection test with flying colors, coming in at a total price of $1085 (shipping included). Final savings at Better Homes. $638.40. Alright! Other lines available are Bassett (cribs and youth groups), Broyhill, and Stanley. To order, you need to send a deposit check of 25% first, then send the balance in a certified check prior to delivery (financing is offered). Shippers are paid upon delivery. Better Homes has been in business since 1917 and guarantees satisfaction.

Boyles Distinctive Furniture
616 Greensboro Road
P.O. Box 958
Highpoint, NC 27261
(910) 884-8088

Hours: Mon.–Wed. 8:30–5:30;
Thurs.–Fri. 8:30–8:30;
Sat. 8:30–5:30
Payment: Checks, MC, Visa, financing available
Publications available: brochure and store mailer

Boyles gets high marks for handling one of our favorite children's furniture lines, Thomasville, whose Ribbons & Bows collection in antique washed pine with true dovetail joints and 20-step finishing process is a real show-stopper. However, you must have visited the Boyles showroom in person within 90 days to purchase items from the Thomasville line.

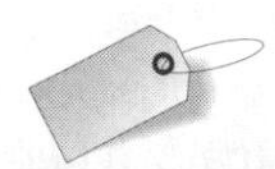

Bargain Byte

You'll never need to pay retail prices for furniture as long as Highpoint, North Carolina remains in the Union. Highpoint is the furniture capital of the United States. This is where the leading decorating and home furnishings editors from major magazines and newspapers go to check out the latest trends and designs in the furniture industry. Highpoint is also where smart consumers go, either in person or by phone, to buy fine furniture at discounts up to 70% off list prices! Even with the delivery charges, you still save a minimum of 30% to 40% off most suggested retail prices. We've done it and dozens of other smart shoppers have told us that going to Highpoint is the only way to buy furniture!

Cherry Hill Furniture

Mail order only
P.O. Box 7405
Furnitureland Station
High Point, NC 27264
(800) 328-0933
(800) 888-0933
(910) 882-0933

Hours: Mon.–Sat. 9–6
Payment: Cashier's checks, money orders, personal checks
Publications available: store mailer

Cherry Hill is a one-stop discount shop where you can mail-order everything for your child's room—wall-to-wall carpet, accent pieces, collectibles, area rugs, mirrors, wall art, lighting, and of course, furniture at up to 50% off list price and more. One problem: getting through on the toll-free numbers is difficult, so we ended up making the long-distance calls. Cherry Hill carries the usual Lexington, Lea, and Bassett baby and juvenile furniture plus Broyhill. Cherry Hill has no showroom, and the company doesn't send out manufacturer brochures. Decide on what you want by visiting local retailers. Then call Cherry Hill with your best price quote, manufacturer model numbers, and color numbers. Cherry Hill then gives you its best price.

Coffey Discount Furniture

Hwy. 321—Poovey Drive
P.O. Box 141
Granite Falls, NC 28630
(704) 396-2900 (phone)
(704) 396-3050 (fax)

Hours: Mon.–Sat. 9–5
Payment: Personal and cashier's checks only
Publications available: mailer and catalogs

Prices here are pretty good, roughly 10% over cost, 50% off retail. However, the sales help was less than friendly and not very knowledgeable. When we inquired about juvenile lines available, they told us about Bassett only. What about Lexington, Stanley, and Lea? We seemed to have jolted the sales people out of their coma with that question, and they replied that they did represent those lines, but that Lexington was limited in its youth groups. Since when? Despite the reps' low furniture I.Q., we're including them in our listing just to give you another resource for pricing purposes. Orders here must be placed in writing.

Enchanted Heirlooms
P.O. Box 414
Lookout Mountain, TN 37350
(800) 615-4299

Hours: seven days a week, 24 hours
Payment: Visa, MC, Discover, Diners, checks
Publications available: discount catalog

I fell in love with Enchanted Heirlooms after seeing their exquisite, handpainted dollhouse loft bed for girls and Coach Kleats Collection locker-room loft bed for boys at a furniture show. Unfortunately, these pieces had "lofty" price tags as well. Today, though, you can buy factory direct through the company's catalog division and save from 30% to 70% off suggested retail on this dreamland stuff for kids!

You can order pieces for the nursery, including a wicker basket and old-fashioned rocker, up through big girl and big boy twin beds in coordinating wicker or wood. Choose from an assortment of color schemes with or without delightful handpainting (pick theirs or custom design your own). Dressers, desks, vanity tables, play area groups, mirrors, and even custom comforters, pillow shams, and dust ruffles are available. This company can customize pieces to match pre-existing fabrics and wallpaper, including your own fabrics.

Furniture Collections of Carolina
Route 8, Box 128
Hwy 127 South Mt. View
Hickory, NC 28602
(704) 294-3593

Hours: Mon.–Sat. 9–5:30
Payment: Visa, MC
Publications available: brochures and mailers

A separate baby furniture gallery distinguishes this outlet from the rest. In fact, this outlet is one of the very few to sell Childcraft cribs, dressers, and changing tables at discount prices. Other baby lines showcased here include Welsh, Simmons, and Bassett. Juvenile groupings feature Broyhill, Stanley, Lexington, Lea, and Bassett at 20% to 50% off suggested retail prices. You also can find a selection of wooden high chairs by Simmons, plus cradles. Deliveries to 48 states.

J.E. Hudson Discount Furniture
940 Highland Ave.
P.O. Box 2547
Hickory, NC 28601
(704) 322-4996
(704) 322-5717
(704) 322-6953 (fax)

Hours: Mon.–Sat. 8:30–5
Payment: MC, Visa, checks
Publications available: brochures and mailer

Hudson's has been in business for over 75 years and has a 20,000-square-foot showroom. The *Atlanta Constitution* describes Hudson's as "the outlet that offers one of the best discounts we found." Indeed, one salesperson claimed that Lexington furniture is discounted up to 70% off suggested retail prices.

Hudson's is the largest volume dealer for Sealy Posturepedic mattresses, so expect substantial reductions even with freight charges. To begin, go to your local Sealy dealer, choose the mattress you want, and get the specific name of that item (the name under the word *Posturepedic*). Also ask the salesperson for the level number (numbers go as high as 9). This number assists in decoding the mattress of your choice.

Hudson's carries additional lines for babies, children, and teens including Stanley, Broyhill, Baby Bassett, and Vaughan-Bassett. Hudson's sells on a wholesale-plus basis that comes to a 40% to 50% savings off most manufacturers' retail prices.

Loftin Black
(800) 334-7398
111 Sedgehill Drive
Thomasville, NC 27360

Hours: Mon.–Fri. 8:30–5:30;
Sat. 8:30–5
Payment: Visa, MC, Discover
Publications available: brochures and store mailer

Loftin is one of the few furniture outlets that still has a toll-free number. You will need manufacturers' names, model numbers, color numbers, catalog number, fabric number, and fabric grades when you call. Loftin discounts 35% to 50% on Lexington, Stanley, Lea, and Bassett. We put Loftin Black to the Betsy Cameron Children's Collection test (see Shaw Furniture Gallery) and here are the prices: $1,100 total price for Casey's Cupboard and Daddy's Girl dresser (shipping, uncartoning, and setup included). Shaw prices were $1,186—not bad, but so far, Loftin Black is the big winner. Recall that a leading furniture store in my area was asking $1723.40 complete with shipping and tax for both pieces. I'm happy saving $623—wouldn't you be?

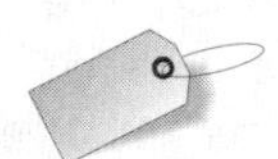

Bargain Byte

If you're planning a trip to North Carolina, you should know about the wonderful perks offered by many of the outlets and furniture galleries in and around the Highpoint area. Based on minimum dollars spent, which varies from outlet to outlet, you may be entitled to free accommodations, complimentary tours, dinners, airfare vouchers, golf fees, frequent flyer mileage, and more! Remember to inquire about sale-motivated promotions when you call.

Murrow Furniture Galleries
3514 South College Road
P.O. Box 4337
Wilmington, NC 28406
(910) 799-4010

Payment: Visa, MC, checks, cash
Publications available: brochures and store mailer

This outlet gallery specializes in interior design and great prices on fine furniture. Fax your floor plans to Murrow and you can get free design assistance. Childcraft cribs and youth furniture are featured here at 30% off suggested retail prices. Those famous glider-rockers and ottomans by Dutailier of Canada are available at about 40% off list prices! You'd have to be off your rocker to buy them at your local, fully retail, juvenile furniture shop! Other popular furniture lines include Stanley, Lexington, Lea Industries, Simmons, Thomasville (in-store purchases only, but Murrow ships anywhere), and others at 25% to 40% off retail. The store also stocks Serta bedding and Kingsdown baby crib mattresses (used by hospitals because of the special treatment to prevent staph infections).

Murrow urges customers to inspect its furniture by pulling out the units to look at the back and interior. The store advises people to reject any piece assembled with staples.

By the way, Murrow's 45,000-square-foot showroom is only 10 minutes away from a beautiful resort area, so you may want to think about planning your vacation and furniture shopping at the same time.

Nite Furniture Company
611 S. Green St.
Morgantown, NC 28655
(704) 437-1491

Hours: Mon.–Fri. 9–6;
Sat. 9–5:30
Payment: Cash, personal checks
Publications available: brochure and mailer

This city block (80,000 square feet) of the best-made furniture in America is divided into three showroom buildings. The designers here can help you coordinate everything for your child's room including the furniture, wall coverings, lamps, fabrics, bedspreads, carpets, and rugs. Prices on Lexington and Stanley furniture range from 35% to 50% off list prices.

Shaw Furniture Galleries
Clearance Center
2017 South College Road
Highpoint, NC 27260
(910) 498-2628 (phone)
(910) 498-7889 (fax)

Hours: Mon.–Sat. 9–5:30
Payment: Visa, MC

Outlet
P.O. Box 576
Randelman, NC 27317

Hours: Mon.–Fri. 9–5:30
Payment: Visa, MC
Publications available: brochures and store mailer

This major discounter, in business for 56 years, purchases in volume, operates on a small profit margin, and ships almost every conceivable furniture line anywhere at 30% to 50% off suggested retail. Do your shopping homework and then call Shaw with manufacturer model numbers (including the color numbers) and your best price. You get an immediate price quote over the phone. (You don't have to stay on hold, accumulating a long-distance phone bill; Shaw calls you right back).

Order the store mailer, which lists many of the furniture companies they represent, but keep in mind that the list is not complete. Because of competition among retailers, many furniture companies prohibit North Carolina outlets from advertising or sending brochures by mail. Discount selling policies vary among the companies. For example, if you want to purchase Thomasville from Shaw, you need to have bought from Shaw before (time limitations may apply), or you need to come to Shaw in person or have a referral from someone who has purchased from Shaw. Most companies don't have such rigid restrictions, but if the line you're interested in isn't in the mailer, ask Shaw if it's available. Seek and ye shall find . . . great bargains, that is!

We decided to put Shaw to the test and gauge how cost-effective, cooperative, and informative the company really is. According to the store mailer, the staff at Shaw consists of sales reps and interior designers. We went to Shaw with what we thought would be quite a challenge. One of the more delightful and exclusive entries in kids' furniture suites comes from Lexington's Betsy Cameron Children's Collection. These dramatic-looking pieces, described as *investment quality* furnishings, feature handpainted appliqués, double bunk and trundle units draped with tie-back curtains, sleigh beds, canopy beds, antique-looking handpainted cribs, armoires, computer hutches, school girl

Bargain Byte

Thou shalt not shop by catalog alone! If you follow the advice in this chapter, you will be inundated with catalogs from every manufacturer that produces juvenile furniture. But don't get too excited yet. Photographers and their trusty stylists are wizards at making even the cheapest furniture look expensive and exquisite. Don't buy anything until you have seen it, touched it, and inspected it in person. You need to physically shake beds for flimsiness, pull out drawers to see if they're big enough and easy enough to pull out, judge the quality and strength of the wood (is it too light in feel for your satisfaction?), and check out the paint. If you don't know where to see the line you're interested in, call the company directly and ask for customer service. Ask for the names of dealers or stores in your area.

desks, swivel mirrors with flip-side bulletin boards, dream-like vanity tables, and upholstered candy-stash stools.

My choices were Casey's Cupboard, outfitted with antique-lace, fabric-panel inserts, TV compartment, clothes rods, three shelves, three drawers, and beveled mirror; and Daddy's Girl Dresser, featuring four drawers (one with a lock and felt-lined), wood knob drawer pulls, and handpainted appliqué flowers. The local branch of a popular furniture chain quoted prices (exclusive of special sale days) at $999 for the cupboard and $549 for the dresser, plus a $50 delivery and set-up charge. Add my local sales tax of $125.40, and the grand total was $1723.40. Shaw's prices: $687 for the cupboard, $344 for the dresser, and a delivery and set-up charge of $155. With no tax from North Carolina, the total cost was $1,186. I saved $537.40 by purchasing the set from Shaw!

Service-wise, Shaw's representatives displayed good old-fashioned southern hospitality and were knowledgeable and exceedingly helpful. In fact, once the salesperson got a handle on my tastes, she recommended other lines that were similar in design and less expensive!

Shaw even has a clearance center where you can purchase samples, canceled orders, closeouts, and discontinueds at dealer's cost or less. You must shop in person; the clearance center has no mail order.

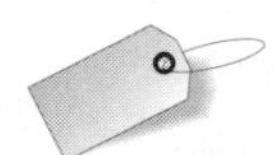

Bargain Byte

Many parents make North Carolina a vacation destination and actually rent a truck to transport furniture bargains. Or if you're on your way to or from Florida, you can simply pull off the interstate for a two- or three-day shopping spree. Then you can have your pick of all brands, including the lines with restrictions such as Thomasville.

Stuckey Brothers Furniture Company

Route 1, Box 527
Stuckey, NC 29554
(803) 558-2591 (phone)
(803) 558-9229 (fax)

Hours: Mon.–Fri. 9–6; Sat. 9–5
Payment: Personal checks
Publications available: brochures and mailer

We give the fax number for this company because you actually need to place your order in writing, indicating style number, finish, fabric information, and quantity. Stuckey's delivery system is impeccable; it has a double-check system to ensure quality control with each piece uncrated and inspected. You can find discounts up to 45% on Moosehead, Lexington, Stanley, Vaughan, Vaughan-Bassett, and Lea Industries.

On our continuing quest for the latest in handpainted furniture, Stuckey recommended we take a look at Lea's Victoria's Garden. The antique bisque finish is complemented with a decal of pastel ribbons, flowers, and green leaves. The collection is constructed of pine solids and features vertical dovetailed joints along with lock joints on drawer backs for reinforced strength. The beautiful decals are featured on all pieces, including sleigh bed with trundle, tester bed, panel bed, nightstands, hutch mirror, drawer chests, and student desks. Lea also manufactures a Back Country rodeo bed collection for boys in medium rustic pine finish with antique and twisted gun metal bails.

Triad Furniture Discounters

P.O. Box 7509
Myrtle Beach, SC 29577-9806
(800) 323-8469

Hours: Mon.–Fri. 4–6; Sat. 9–5
Payment: Visa, MC, Discover
Publications available: brochures and mailer

Expect to save around 40% on top children's lines here including Bassett (no cribs, however), Broyhill, Lexington, and Stanley. Triad's *tell-a-friend program* can earn you additional discounts up to 25% off future purchases. Keep in mind that the friend needs to request your salesperson and mention the referral.

Young's Furniture and Rug Company
1706 North Main Street
P.O. Box 5005
Highpoint, NC 27262
(910) 883-4111

Hours: Mon.–Sat. 9–5:30
Payment: Most major credit cards
Publications available: brochure and store mailer

Although this company basically carries only the Lexington line for kids, we found Young's prices to be among the most competitive in North Carolina. In business for over 48 years, Young's claims its discounts are more than 45% off regular retail. You may want to wait for Young's annual winter sale that offers additional discounts of 5% to 10% off its already reduced merchandise, including Lexington. Young's ships anywhere in the U.S. and guarantees satisfaction upon delivery.

Mid-Atlantic Region

Carolina Furniture of Williamsburg
5425 Richmond Road
Williamsburg, VA 23188
(804) 565-3000

Hours: Mon.–Thurs., Sat. 9–6; Sun. 1–6
Payment: Visa, MC
Publications available: store mailer

We finally found a furniture outlet store that doesn't appear to have any restrictions on ordering Thomasville furniture at discount. If you have been searching for that Ribbons & Bows group that Thomasville does so well, or any other youth collection, here's what you need to do. Stop by your local Thomasville Gallery store and gather up brochures from the groups you're interested in. If for some reason you cannot get the pamphlets, make sure you know the exact name and prices of the group, and be prepared to describe the pieces in detail (number of drawers, color, hardware, appliqué designs, type of bed, dimensions etc.). Thomasville brochures do not include model numbers. Armed and ready, you can now call a salesperson at Carolina Furniture for price quotes and ordering information. In addition to Thomasville, this company can get Lexington and Stanley juvenile and teen furniture. Discounts range from 40% to 60% off suggested retail prices, and the company ships anywhere.

New England Region

In the historic furniture-making town of Gardner, Massachusetts, ("chair city of the world"), you can find five enormous outlets offering 35% to 40% off list prices on name-brand furniture and accessories for babies, children, and teens. Unfortunately, the deliveries are limited to the surrounding New England states only. If you live in Maine, Vermont, Rhode Island, Connecticut, or Massachusetts, you're in luck! Of course, if you're industrious, you can always rent a trailer.

Copeland Furniture Outlet
Main Street
Bradford, VT 05033
(802) 222-5300
(802) 222-9282 (for appointments)

Hours: Vary (see below)
Payment: Visa, MC
Publications available: store mailer

Copeland designs and manufactures contemporary hardwood furniture seen in such specialty stores as Crate 'n' Barrel, Storehouse, Room and Board, Our House, and Abodio. The factory store offers everyday discounts of 25% to 30% off the lowest retail prices on minor defect seconds and pre-production prototypes that never made it into the line. This furniture is top-notch, solid maple and solid cherry, for the most discriminating tastes. Store hours vary throughout the year so it's best to call first. Copeland can set up private appointments on the days the store is closed.

The Factory Coop
45 Logan St.
Gardner, MA 01440
(508) 632-1447

Hours: Mon.–Fri. 9–5; Sat. 9–6; Sun. 12–5
Payment: MC, Visa, Discover, checks, cash
Publications available: store mailer

Again, The Factory Coop restricts deliveries to the immediate New England states. However, the company carries Lexington and Stanley youth furniture groups at up to 40% off retail prices. Take exit 23 and get off at Route 2.

Lachances's Gardner Furniture Outlet
25 Kraft St.
Gardner, MA 01440
(508) 632-9661
(800) 828-5556 (Residents of MA only)

Hours: Mon.–Wed., Sat. 8–5; Thurs., Fri. 8–8; Sun. 12–5
Payment: Visa, MC, Discover, checks, cash
Publications available: brochure (call 508 632-1436)

Find Lexington, Stanley, and Vermont Tubbs children's groups at up to 40% reductions at the Gardner Furniture Outlet. Vermont Tubbs features bunk beds, twin beds, dressers, student desks, and more in solid ash. Sturdy stuff, this Vermont Tubbs. Take exit 22 and get off at Route 2.

Marden's
Surplus and Salvage
(207) 873-6111 (call for the seven Maine locations)

Hours: Mon.–Fri 9–8; Sat. 9–5; Sun. 12–5
Payment: Visa, MC, Discover

This way off-price business claims to have stock of virtually every brand of children's furniture at some time. Marden's has first-quality, department store overstocks and merchandise salvaged from earthquakes, hurricanes, and tornadoes at 40% to 70% off retail prices.

You'll be blown away by these prices for top furniture brands in daybeds, cribs, flooring, kid recliners, dressers, and more.

R. Smith Furniture Co.
289 South Main St.
Gardner, MA 01440
(508) 632-3461

Hours: Mon.–Thurs., Sat. 8–5; Fri. 8–8; Sun. 1–5
Payment: MC, Visa, Discover, personal checks, cash
Publications available: brochures and mailer

This company specializes in colonial and traditional styles. If you're interested in furniture constructed the way master cabinetmakers of the 18th century made furniture, you may want to examine The Moosehead Collection.
This furniture has mortise and tenon joints on the dust panels, and tilt-proof, dovetailed drawers with built-in drawer stops to protect tiny toes from getting smashed. Made from select northern hardwoods, Moosehead manufacturers tell us that these pieces are so solid, they can easily be handed down from generation to generation. In fact, the same rock maple that is used for ballroom floors, basketball courts, and bowling lanes is what Moosehead uses in combination with yellow birch to craft children's cribs, dressers, and beds. Although your kids probably won't dance or bowl on the furniture, it's nice to know they can, if the urge, um, strikes. You can find Moosehead at R. Smith at discounts of 35% below suggested retail prices. Visit the bargain room on the second floor for more treasures.

Winchendon Furniture Co.
13 Railroad St.
Winchendon, MA 01475
(508) 297-0131

Hours: Tues.–Thurs., Sat. 9–5:30; Fri. 9–8; Sun. 1–5
Payment: Visa, Discover, MC, checks, cash
Publications available: brochures and mailer

The staff at this outlet was most courteous and sent us practically every brochure on baby and juvenile collections from Lexington. The outlet also represents Moose-head solid maple cribs and youth suites. Expect to find discounts here up to 45%. During the month of January, take an extra 10% off on floor samples. Winchendon is on route 2 off exit 24.

New York Tri-State Area

Baby Club of America Warehouse Outlet and Catalog
721 Campbell Ave.
West Haven, CT 06516
(800) 752-9736 (800-PLAY-PEN)
(203) 931-7760

Hours: Mon.–Wed. 10–6; Thurs. and Fri. 10–9; Sat. 10–6; Sun. 12–5
Payment: Visa, MC, AmEx, Discover, checks, cash
Publications available: catalog

Thought you couldn't find Perego, Aprica, Emmaljunga, and MacLaren strollers at discounted prices? Ta-Da! Here they are! Thought you'd never find those exquisite, contemporary Ragazzi cribs at discounted prices? Ta-Da again!

The Baby Club of America offers a full array of products including strollers, playpens, car seats, baby carriers, high chairs, baby monitors, baby video monitors, cribs, port-a-cribs, youth beds, bunk beds, and accessories at 20%–40% off suggested retail prices.

At the warehouse outlet you can find the aforementioned

Ragazzi cribs along with Childcraft and Evenflo juvenile furniture. Baby Club also offers top-of-the-line bedding to go with its beautiful cribs and beds. Inquiring minds want to know which lines these would be, so pardon our name dropping: Glenna Jean, California Baby, Lambs & Ivy, Brandee Danielle, Cotton Tales, Red Calliope, Judi's Originals, Patsy Aiken, House of Hatten, Nojo, Carousel, Quiltcraft, Quiltex, Kidsline, Clothwork, Forever Children, and more to come, they tell us! Most bedding collections include comforters, sheets, bumpers, wall hangings, diaper stackers, musical mobiles, dust ruffles, rocking chair pads, changing table pads and covers, quilted blankets, cradle sets, canopies, fabric by the yard, decorative pillows, window treatments, and highchair pads—whew! Again, the entire stock is 20%–40% off suggested retail prices.

For shoppers who cannot get to the outlet, you can receive Baby Club's catalog and order via mail or phone, anything the store carries at the same discounts. Baby Club also has a membership club, where for an annual fee of $25 (you can sign up three "associates" for free under your membership), you are entitled to take an additional 10% off the low, blue-colored price in the catalog. Additional membership services include free educational/financial planning for the family; a quarterly newsletter listing product recalls and health/safety articles; a baby shower registry; birth announcement mailing service; and exclusive member sales and closeouts.

Here's one example of how terrific this place really is. For the top-of-the-line Perego "Milano" stroller, you would pay around $400 at a full-price specialty store; at Baby Club, the stroller sells for $299, and with the membership discount, your final cost comes down to $269. Since it's almost impossible to buy this line of strollers at a discount, this reduction is great!

Bloomingdales Furniture Clearance Center
155 Glen Cove Road
Carle Place, NY 11514
(516) 294-3410

Hours: Mon.–Fri. 10–9:30; Sat. 10–6; Sun. 12–5
Payment: Visa, MC, AmEx

Bloomingdales Clearance Center is a wonderful place to haunt and hunt for furniture bargains you might otherwise never consider due to the high department store price. On occasion, the Bloomies Clearance Center gets some children's pieces, so it doesn't hurt to investigate from time to time. What the store does have on hand most of the time, however, are twin mattresses from Serta, Stearns & Foster, Shifman, and other reputable bedding names. Discounts at the store range from 25% to 60% off retail. Additional sales throughout the year target specific sections of the store and bring prices down further. Bloomingdales accepts phone orders, but keep in mind that all sales are final.

North Carolina Furniture Showrooms
12 West 21st St.
New York, NY 10010
(212) 260-5850

Hours: Mon.–Sat. 10–6; Sun. 12–5
Payment: Visa, MC, AmEx, checks
Publications available: store mailer

If you know exactly what you want for your kids, including manufacturer name and style, then you may want to give these furniture guys a try because they guarantee they won't be undersold! We were pleased to see that not only does this company carry the obligatory Bassett, Broyhill, Lea, Stanley, and Lexington, but it also has begun stocking I.D.

Kids, which is reputed to be one of the best children's formica furniture lines in the business. You can choose from an assortment of colors and hardware finishes in I.D. Kids. Expect average discounts on kids' lines to range from 30%–45% off suggested retail prices.

Mattresses from Sealy, Serta, Simmons, and Stearns & Foster are also available here at 40% to 50% off. Bring the sales people as much information as you can find off the mattress ticket from a retail store (including level number). The staff can decode the number for you and procure the same product at substantial savings!

If you make a purchase from North Carolina Furniture Showrooms, an on-staff decorator can assist you in room planning at no extra charge. Unfortunately, the store cannot provide you with brochures, so shop around, then give them a call or a visit.

Midwestern Region

District Factory Outlet

125 East North St.
Decatur, IL 62523
(217) 422-6503

Hours: Mon.–Fri. 10–6;
Sat. 10–5; Sun 12–4

Kids need to relax after a long hard day at school or the playground. Wouldn't they love to fall into their own upholstered kiddie recliner? Or how about a mini sofa, loveseat, and coordinating chair? You can pick up a pint-sized recliner here for $58, or two pieces of coordinated upholstered seating for $99 (about 30% off list price). District also carries twin mattresses and beds for kids' rooms at around 25% off retail.

Cosco Outlet Stores

Factory Direct
13–149 East Hamilton Commons
Noblesville, IN 46060
(317) 770-0693

Hours: Mon.– Sat. 10–6;
Sun. 12–6
Mail/phone orders accepted

3160 Columbus Center
Columbus, IN 47203
(812) 375-5800

Hours: Mon.–Sat. 10–7;
Fri. 10–9
Payment: Visa, MC, Discover

Cosco to go! Baby, do we have some savings for you! Shop your local juvenile furniture stores and jot down style, color, and manufacturer model numbers of any Cosco items you like. Then call the factory outlets and save up to 50% on first-quality and second-quality cribs, car seats, high chairs, play yards, booster seats, changing tables, baby monitors, etc. From May to September, Cosco holds big clearance sales when you can save up to 60% off.

This End Up

Factory Outlet
Gurnee Mills
6170 West Grand Ave.
Gurnee, IL 60031
(847) 855-1601

Hours: Mon.–Sat. 10–9;
Sun. 11–6
Payment: Visa, MC, Discover, AmEx

Located one hour outside of Chicago and Milwaukee, this gem of an outlet can save you 20% to 80% off retail prices (in conjunction with special sales). The company carries very solid, all-wood children's collections and home furnishings. You can find bunk beds, dressers, desks, tables, and chairs made from southern yellow pine in an assortment of shades including cherry (dark), honey-pine, and white-washed (off-white). Southern yellow pine is one of the sturdier, denser woods and wears better than others. This End Up also has a great home furnishings line consisting of comforters, duvets, window treatments, and more at substantial discounts off the catalog prices. (Normal discounts here range from 20%–50% off the catalog prices.) Some drawbacks: the furniture comes unassembled and you need to transport goods yourself (no deliveries). However, most folks have no trouble getting the unassembled pieces in their cars, station wagons, or four-wheel drives. All sales are final.

Welsh Outlet Store
1535 South 8th St.
St. Louis, MO 63104
(314) 231-8828

Hours: Mon.–Fri. 8–4:30; Saturday 9–5
Payment: Visa, MC, checks, cash

For those of you familiar with the St. Louis area, this terrific outlet store for Welsh baby furnishings is right next to Soulard's Farmer's Market—yum! You can save a bundle for your little bundle on cribs, changing tables, dressers, bedding, strollers, and accessories. Styles run the gamut from contemporary to Early American. Prices are a minimum of 20% off retail. Looking for an inexpensive travel umbrella stroller? You can find them here for $10. The outlet store also carries "as-is" cribs for $80 and first-quality cribs topping out at $199 (beats those $700 prices any day).

West Region

Baby On A Budget Discount Mail-Order
PO Box 35434
Houston, TX 77035
(800) 575-2224

Is there any other way to have a baby these days, than on a budget? Here's a real insider shopping secret. If it's nursery necessities you're after—including comforters, quilts, linens, bumpers, dust ruffles, mobiles, lamps and accessories—here's what you do: Shop your local department stores and baby boutiques and jot down brand names, style numbers and pattern descriptions of your favorite items. Baby On A Budget can get you anything you fancy from Glenna Jean to Sweet Pea at 25% off and more. And, Baby On A Budget hasn't forgotten those mommy-relaxing Dutailier glider-rockers—offering them at some of the lowest prices around. You'll also find a selection of premium-brand strollers here such as Aprica and Combi at discounted prices.

Eddie Gold Furniture
4935 McConnell Ave., Bldg. 3
Los Angeles, CA 90066
(213) 870-3050

Hours: Tues.–Fri. 9–5; Sat. 11–5
Payment: Visa, MC, Discover, checks, cash
Publications available: brochures

Naturally, the most glamorous-looking furniture for kids is available in Los Angeles. You can purchase stock or special-ordered items at prices about 40% off suggested retail prices. Manufacturers include Stanley (ask about Stanley's Cottage Bouquet line for girls—it's adorable), Lexington, Lea, and Berg (this southern California line has a great-looking rainbow collection for contemporary tastes). Eddie Gold will be happy to send you catalogs, brochures, and photostats on a request basis. This family-run business has been around for 45 years and ships anywhere in the United States.

JC Penney Outlet
1900 Timberlake
South Arlington, TX 77010
(817) 640-0631

Hours: Mon.–Sat. 10–7
Payment: Major credit cards, checks

Although this location is the main distribution center for Penney's, a separate outlet is at the end of the building. Inventory is constantly changing but from time to time it includes some cribs and youth groups from Bassett, Stanley, and Broyhill. Discounts range from 40% to 60% off suggested retail on these floor samples, discontinued models, and damaged goods, along with some first-quality canceled orders.

Accessories

American Blind, Wallpaper & Carpet Factory
909 N. Sheldon Rd.
Plymouth, MI 48170
(800) 735-5300

Hours: Mon.–Fri. 8–1;
Sat. and Sun. 8–noon
Payment: Visa, MC, Discover, AmEx, checks
Items available: mailers, instructionals, sample kits

Are you interested in saving up to 65% off carpet, 80% off wallpaper, and up to 82% off decorator blinds? We put American to *The Smart Shopper's Guide* test, and here's what we discovered. Our first call to the company got us carpet portfolios, a wallpaper catalog, and a comprehensive shades and blinds kit with real metal, plastic, and fabric samples. Very impressive, but not as impressive as the price quotes we got. I've had my eye on some new pleated shades from Hunter Douglas called "A Shade Younger," designed with colorful patterns such as ragtime dolls, dinosaurs, toy trains, and balloons. At retail, the ragtime dolls 57"×42" pleated shade costs $412. American quoted $85.91 for the same item.

The wallpaper catalog was a bit too limited and predictable for my taste, but you don't have to rely on the catalog alone. You can choose any wallpaper (Laura Ashley to Ralph Lauren) from your local store and call with the book name, pattern number, description of wallpaper, and page number. Chances are, American can get the wallpaper for you at up to 80% off retail. Bonuses from this company include free shipping, no tax, and free premium padding for all carpet orders. By the way, a free U.S. Savings Bond offer came with the sample kits. You get a $50 bond with a minimum purchase of $250, and a $100 bond with minimum purchase of $500. (Only one savings bond per household.)

National Blind & Wallpaper Factory
400 Galleria
Suite 400
Southfield, MI 48034
(800) 477-8000

Hours: Mon.–Fri. 8am–midnight; Sat. and Sun. 8am–10pm
Payment: all major credit cards
Publications available: mailers, brochures, samples

National sends out terrific sample sets. The company sells double honeycomb custom cellular shades at up to 75% off; mini and micro aluminum blinds are up to 80% off; 1", 2", 3" custom wood blinds are up to 75% off; and vertical blinds and pleated shades in designer fabric and vinyl collections are up to 75% off retail. All you need to do is select your blind type and color, and measure carefully. For wallpaper, this company encourages you to shop locally and record the book number, pattern number, and manufacturer. Ask your installer how many rolls you need, then call National. Don't worry about altered pattern numbers; the folks at National claim they can decode most numbers. You have no hidden shipping costs, no sales tax on orders outside of Michigan, no processing fees, and quick turnaround.

Don't Get Fleeced Getting the Best Deal at Your Next White Sale

Did you know that only 50 years ago fitted sheets weren't around? You made sheets by ordering fabric from a local merchant and sewing them up yourself. Today, you have an overwhelming selection of colors, fabrics, textures, and a home furnishings vocabulary that's almost impossible to decipher. The bottom line is that all bedding and sheets, especially children's, are not created equally. Here's a guide to help navigate your way through the next white sale:

- *Thread count*—The number of threads per square inch. (Hold the sheet up to the light. If you can see through the fabric and make out the actual weave, you're dealing with a low thread count. Put the sheet back.) A high thread count indicates a higher percentage of cotton is present, making for a softer feel and higher price. Higher thread counts produce a better quality sheet with a silkier "hand feel." Anything above a 250 TC (thread count) is considered a high-end luxury sheet.

- *Combed cotton*—A cleaning process that eliminates impurities and short, less desirable fibers to create a smooth and stronger yarn.

- *Easy care/durable press*—These goods have been chemically or mechanically treated to reduce wrinkling.

- *Deep pockets*—Pay attention! There's nothing worse than bringing home a brand new fitted sheet, only to find that you can't pull a sheet corner over the mattress. To avoid this annoyance, look for the words *deep pocket* or a specific measurement (preferably 10 1/2", not 8 1/2") on fitted sheet packages. This term refers to the sheet's box depth. When purchasing irregular or second sheets, keep in mind that incorrect sizing may be the reason for the sharp reduction in price. Ask a salesperson if this is the case. Better yet, see if you can remove the sheet and measure it just to make sure.

- *Muslin*—Often used on character theme bedding for kids, muslin is considered to be the low end of the cotton spectrum. Manufactured with extra-heavy dyes necessary for the printing process, the result is one rough and tough sheet. Expect to find TCs of 128–140 in muslins.
- *Percale*—A smooth, flat, closely woven and combed fabric. Percales come in 100% cotton or 50/50 cotton/polyester blends. Percale is a finer and more tightly woven fabric than muslin. Expect to find TCs of 180–200 in the percales.
- *Pima or Supima*—A high-quality cotton whose long fiber staple is somewhat similar to that of Egyptian cotton. The differences are merely geographical. Pima is grown in the southwestern part of the U.S. and Egyptian is grown along the Nile River. Supima is a fabric made from extra-long staple pima. A lovely, soft "hand feel" makes pima and supima very desirable in bedding. Expect to find TCs of 200–250.
- *Egyptian cotton*—This is the cotton queen of the Nile. Grown alongside the river, Egyptian is the ultimate cotton due to its extra-long fiber staple that creates superior durability, luster, and silky-soft "hand feel." Expect TCs of 200–300.

Rest comfortably knowing that a $60 designer sheet made out of 100% combed pima cotton with a thread count of 250 is no different than a non-designer 250 TC pima sheet for $30. In fact, many designers lend their names to the big mills and have little, if anything, to do with the actual design process.

Buy American and you can save big bucks. Import duties and transportation fees can quadruple the price of an imported sheet. Egyptian cotton sheets manufactured abroad can run as much as $300 to $500 per sheet once they hit American shores. Look for Egyptian and pimas manufactured in the U.S. for more reasonable prices. (See the Kar-Elle listing.)

To save additional dollars on sheets, stick to white goods. Solid colors are more expensive than whites, and printed sheets with dyed backgrounds cost more than prints on white grounds. Keep in mind that each color requires its own screen, so the more colors used, the costlier the sheet. Added embellishments such as piping, scalloped edges, embroidery, and lace also raise the price.

With the average lifespan of a sheet 10 to 15 years, it makes good dollars and sense to wrap your kids in luxury and buy better quality sheets for comfort, durability, and beauty. The following section tells you how to do it on the cheap.

Best Bedding Buys

Anichini Outlet Store
Powerhouse Mall
West Lebanon, NH 03784
(603) 298-8656

Hours: Mon.–Sat. 10–9; Sun 12–5
Payment: Visa, MC, Discover, AmEx

Anichini bed, bath, and table linens rank right up there in the same heirloom quality category as Pratesi and Porthault. The Bambini Anichini bedding collection, imported from Italy, is carried in such uppercrust retailers as Barney's, ABC Carpet, Neiman Marcus, and Bergdorf Goodman. At the outlet store you can choose from crib duvets, decorative pillows and cases, twin bedding, and baby linens in antique lace, Egyptian and silk cotton, and quilted/pique textures. The store features incomparable elegance at sensational prices. Prices are wholesale or lower.

Carousel Designs
Factory Store
4519 Bankhead Highway
Douglasville, GA (25 minutes outside Atlanta)
(770) 949-5977

Hours: usually open Saturdays. Call for exact hours and directions.
Payment: cash only

This Carousel really does have its ups and downs with sales. Calling the phone number gives you a recorded message of the days and hours of Carousel's sporadic factory sales. Sale dates are based on how much inventory, overruns, samples, prototypes, and imperfect merchandise has accumulated. Sales generally take place once or twice a month on Fridays and Saturdays. If you're in need of quality crib linens and infant bedding, Carousel is a good resource. Although we're not wild about 50/50 percale blend sheets, some 100% cotton sheets are available. Otherwise, Carousel has a large selection (25 colors) of solid sheets and appliquéd styles, without screen printing. Appliqués come in an assortment of motifs including bunnies, florals, bears, balloons, and more. Naturally, you also can get coordinating comforters, dust ruffles, bumpers, and decorative pillows. Expect to pay around wholesale prices.

House of Hatten Outlet
San Marcos Factory Mall
3939 1–H 35 Suite 725
San Marcos, TX 78666
(512) 392-8161

Hours: Mon.–Sat. 10–9; Sun. 11–6
Payment: Visa, MC, Discover, AmEx
Mail/phone orders accepted

One of the more upscale brands of crib bedding and accessories, House of Hatten designs high-quality embroidered, smocked, and appliquéd cotton furnishings for the nursery. The outlet store offers discontinued but first-quality and slightly imperfect comforters, fitted sheets, bumpers, pillows, diaper stackers, dust ruffles, musical mobiles, and wall hangings at 30% off retail prices. Our fave rave here? The House of Hatten Hearts & Flowers ensemble in all-white with embroidered flower bouquets set in stitched hearts. You can even get matching stuffed bunny rattles and bibs. House of Hatten gladly ships anywhere in the U.S.

Kar-Elle Originals
Factory Store
Regency Plaza
Brodheadsville, PA 18322
(717) 992-5613

Hours: Mon.–Sat. 9–6
Payment: MC, Visa, checks, cash
This store is directly in front of the Kar-Elle factory. Call for payment methods.

Found only in higher-end specialty stores, Kar-Elle is one of the few companies that makes children's sheets in pure Egyptian cotton. Kar-Elle has 200 fabrics to choose from including Irish linen, Swiss lace, satin, chintz, florals, stripes, gingham, denim, and eyelet, all in 100% cotton. Why not treat your sensitive-skin child to a night in silky Egyptian cotton bedding? We particularly love the pristine white sheets with baby-pink rosebud nosegays trimmed with pale green leaves. At retail, this twin sheet would set you back $75. Here, it's about half that. The store sells everything you need for baby through teen years—comforters, dust ruffles, sheets, bumpers, and blankets—at wholesale prices.

Laura Ashley Outlet Stores
(914) 928-4561
Route 32, C–9
Central Valley, NY 10917

Quality Outlet Center
5529 International Drive
Orlando, FL 32819
(407) 351-2785

Rockvale Square
35 South Willowdale Dr.
Box 103
Lancaster, PA 17602
(717) 397-7116

Reading Outlet
830 Oley St.
Reading, PA 19604
(610) 478-9614

Hours: Central Valley store is open Sun.–Wed. 10–6; Thurs.–Sat. 10–8. Call other stores for exact times.
Payment: Visa, MC, AmEx, and their very own Laura Ashley charge card
Phone orders accepted

Laura Ashley prints, fabrics, wallcoverings, and bedding add a refined, decorative look to any baby or child's room. The Castleberry collection has been around forever and is still often used on film/TV shoots and in magazine photos. You can phone order from the outlet stores, where discontinued patterns and seconds with minor imperfections are available. (The salesperson says that 9 out of 10 people cannot detect the problem and don't care once it's pointed out to them.) Savings here range from 25% off on first-quality goods to 50% off on discontinued groups and irregulars. You can find everything including sheets, quilts, wall coverings, borders, and more.

Nojo Company Store
2431 Antonio Parkway
Suite B 190
Rancho Santa Margarita, CA 92688
(714) 858-9496

Hours: Mon.–Sat. 10–6; Sun. 11–7
Payment: Visa, MC, Discover, AmEx
Phone orders accepted

Nojo's new custom bedding collection in Classic Denim, Treasure Chest, and Strawberry Fields is beautifully designed and comes in complete nursery ensembles featuring comforter, natural cotton linens, wall borders, lamp shades, and even musical mobiles. Now you can order first-quality goods like these from the Nojo Company Store and receive 25% off retail. You also can find the famous Nojo baby sling, gifts, fabrics, car seat covers, and all-important car seat inserts for newborns that prevent wobbly heads from flopping around like a rag doll. Discontinued groups and irregular merchandise are reduced up to 50% off retail prices. Orders are shipped anywhere in the world.

Patsy Aiken Factory Stores
4812 Hargrove Road
Raleigh, NC 27604
(919) 872-8789

Cotswold Mall
300-C S. Sharon Amity
Charlotte, NC 28211
(704) 365-3723

803-C Friendly Center Road
Greensboro, NC 27408
(910) 632-9377

Hours: Mon.–Sat. 10–5
Payment: Visa, MC, checks

You can always rely on Patsy Aiken for expertly tailored clothing (see Chapter 1) and bedding items for babies and children. Specializing in appliqué accents from animals to flowers in striking colors and styles, Patsy Aiken is one of the premier lines in room accessories—guaranteed to turn your child's room into a showplace. Here's what you do. If you're going to North Carolina to take advantage of its great furniture deals, schedule a stop to one of the three Patsy Aiken outlet stores where you can pick up headrest bumpers, four-sided bumpers, sheets, quilts, dust ruffles, diaper stackers, stuffed fabric wall hangings, infant seat covers, musical mobiles, lamps and bases, switchplates, and fabrics at 15%–60% off retail prices. Get yourself on the mailing list for advance sale notices and extra price point reductions.

Quiltex Outlet
Factory Store
168 39th St.
Brooklyn, NY 11232
(718) 788-3158

Hours: Mon.–Thurs. 8–4; Fri. 8–1
Free parking at 3901 1st Ave.
Payment: Visa, MC, AmEx

This factory store represents a well-known manufacturer of top-quality bedding and decorative gift items where everything is available at wholesale prices and below. Why register at your local baby boutique when you can come here and get it all (including layette) for half off retail? Quiltex has one of the most comprehensive Beatrix Potter collections we've ever seen including Country Potter, Diamond Potter, Storybook Potter, and Patchwork Potter. All ensembles feature bumpers, pillows, sheets, comforters, diaper stackers, blankets, and diaper bags. Still, our vote for the most outstanding bedding collection went to the Floral Butterfly group in pink and white polka dot back-ground, oversized, pastel-colored butterfly appliqués, eyelet daisies, and tulip accents (this one also has a coordinated wall hanging). Quiltex offers a wide range of novelty style blankets.

Springmaid/Wamsutta Factory Outlet
Massaponax Outlet Center
4852 Southpoint Parkway
Fredericksburg, VA 22407
(540) 898-6579

Phone orders accepted

Tanger Factory Outlet
1770 W. Main St.
Riverhead, NY 11901
(516) 727-7118

(There are approximately 48 factory outlet stores in the U.S. for Springmaid/Wamsutta; check your local outlet malls for the one nearest you.)
Hours: Mon.–Sat. 10–9; Sun.10–7
Payment: Most major credit cards

You can avoid the department stores altogether by phone-ordering most of your children's bedding, and save between 25% and 65% off retail in the process. Start collecting white sale catalogs that come in the mail and look for Springmaid/Wamsutta goods. The factory stores can send you first-quality, discontinued, and irregular merchandise via UPS at incredible savings. Wamsutta's English Rose Gingham twin sheets, with a thread count of 200 and a $3.99 pricetag (around $8 in department stores), are a big hit in my house. The matching comforter goes for $24.99 at the factory stores. For babies, you can find a wide variety of merchandise from outside vendors including Disney character sheets. Many solid flannel sheets are available, plus crib-in-a-bag sets—which include comforter, bumpers, and sheet—for $24.99 in safari and western themes, or pastel and primary palettes.

“”

Look Who's Talking Bargains...To Smart Shoppers
Denise Brodey, lifestyle editor of *Child* magazine

Pay Off-Price for Colors That Went Off the Chart

"Go to your local paint store and ask to see the 'mistints.' These custom colors are usually a paint store's best-kept bargain secret!"

The simplest and cheapest way to spruce up a child's room is to get creative with paints. Your local paint store may have a section devoted to mistints or colors that have been mixed incorrectly, thus rejected by the customer who ordered it. Don't be afraid of these out-of-the-ordinary, bolder, off-chart colors. After all, a child's room is one of the few (if only) places in the house where you can go a little crazy with color.

Today's toxic-free, allergy-free, non-smelling and scrubbable paints (check out Dutch Boy's "Kid Room Paint" for superior dirt resistance—call 800-828-5669 for more information) are ideal for painting kids' rooms and kids' furniture. You can even move the kids back into their rooms on the same day you paint.

Denise also likes Ikea furniture stores for inexpensive and attractive bookends, chairs, stools, and lamps. (One of my more marvelous Ikea finds was a contemporary teal blue halogen desk lamp for $16.)

When it comes to choosing a carpet for your child's room, this Child expert advises, "No deep pile for kids. Keep it flat for optimal playability."

One last money-saving tip from Denise: "You can save extra dollars by declining scotchgarding services when ordering upholstered furniture or custom-ordering quilts and other fabrics. It's a lot cheaper to buy a can and do it yourself. The results are the same."

""

""

Look Who's Talking Bargains…To Smart Shoppers

Sherry Hayslip, interior designer, A.S.I.D., I.I.B.A.

Sherry is the winner of the prestigious American Design Awards: The Hexter Award and Design Ovation Awards. Her work has been featured in countless publications such as Town & Country, Financial Times of London, Christian Science Monitor, *and more.*

Sherry urges parents to take a critical look at unused and discarded furniture items like that old, crummy, heavy oak bachelor chest hidden away in the attic. If it fits in the child's room, consider painting, pickling, or stenciling it.

Save money on expensive wall treatments by copying a popular decorator's trick. Sherry says you can create your own custom stencils for wall borders and furniture enhancement. "First decide on a design concept for the room with your child. Then go to the library and pick out design books and magazines with your chosen motif. Next, blow up your selected designs to full-size on a copy machine and trace the design onto mylar (a heavy plastic you can purchase at an art supply store). Then try this time-tested technique: take a pin and punch holes along the mylar tracing. Position the stencil in place with tape on the wall or furniture, then take a brush and dab graphite powder (again, from your local art supply or paint store) over the holes. Remove the mylar, connect the dots with a pencil, and fill in with paint. It's so easy, anyone can do it.

"Give your child's walls a decorator lift when painting by adding pearlized powder to the color. Iridescent walls lend a beautiful air of fantasy to the room at almost no extra cost. Not all paint stores carry the pearlized powder, but it's worth a few phone calls to track it down."

""

""

Look Who's Talking Bargains...To Smart Shoppers
Mario Buatta, interior designer

What you may not know about this "prince of chintz" is that Mario Buatta has a great affinity and talent for decorating children's rooms. Mario lets us in on some of his innovative, yet inexpensive, do-it-yourself methods for cheering up and beautifying nursery, children's, and teen rooms.

Mario's first money-saving tip: "It's cheaper to decorate with toys than real furnishings! Simply buy several white wicker etageres (bookcases) and display toys all the time. Kids love to look at their possessions, so don't make the mistake of hiding them away."

If you're not comfortable with stenciling walls and furniture, Mario suggests trying decoupage, which also works well on lamps and window shades. Simply cut the design or print of your choice from leftover wallpaper or fabric and glue it to the surface with decoupage glue. (You can find decoupage kits in home furnishing centers and art supply stores.) Finish up with a coat of varnish and you have a great look. You may want to try scattered flowers or ribbons and bows in a girl's room and anything from toy trucks to insects or stripes in a boy's room. You get the picture (the decoupage picture, that is). Mario also likes to use the decoupage technique on unpainted and wicker furniture in children's rooms.

Mario explains that if you like the look of wallpaper but don't want to make the financial investment, you can hang a strip of wallpaper from ceiling to floor (say stripes or flowers) every 12"–14", which opens the room height-wise and gives a taller impression of the room.

Want to try a do-it-yourself canopy? Check out Mario Buatta's own Vogue Butterick Pattern #1731 Wall Drape for $12.50 and create an economical dream bed for your child or teen.

Mario's endquote: "Rag rugs are great for kid rooms. They're cheap, washable, long-lasting, and terrific-looking. They're also a little different from wall-to-wall carpeting that looks so boring."

""

CHAPTER THREE

FIRST-CLASS KIDDIES: TRAVELING LIKE ROYALTY ON A BUDGET

If you're at all like me, you like to fantasize about your family going to the places shown on the travel segments of "Lifestyles of the Rich and Famous." After all, who wouldn't like to experience the wonders of a poolside massage while the kids relocate endangered sea turtle eggs on a beautiful Caribbean beach? Well, you can stop dreaming! Many of these three-, four-, and five-star hotels and resorts are now as affordable as your local motel chain.

After my husband and I started our family, we assumed that traveling with a child meant good-bye Ritz Carlton—hello Motel 6. We couldn't have been more wrong. Luxury hotels are rolling out the child-ready welcome mat for families longing for elegant vacation getaways. The big news: these hotels offer drastically reduced packages that let families with limited vacation dollars experience exceptional facilities and services at affordable rates.

It's true; folks like you and I can indulge in first-class holidays without taking out a second mortgage. The trick is uncovering these special deals. To find a glamorous vacation getaway that doesn't break your budget, you need to take advantage of unpublicized promotions, esoteric airline discounts, low-fare niche airlines, hotel and airline consolidators, coupon books, and club memberships.

First-Class Travel Tips and Caveats

The following list describes the best ways to uncover terrific first-class family vacations at super prices:

- *Be your own travel agent*—Travel agents don't know everything and cannot always plan your trip for less. Travel agents don't always have access to the lowest rates. With a minimal amount of research of your own, you may be able to find a much lower-priced vacation at a significantly more luxurious destination. Although you probably want to begin your research by chatting with an agent, don't stop there. Your next step should be calling the major airlines and inquiring about their promotional deals to your chosen destination. I have found TWA Getaway Vacations (800) 438-2929, Delta Dream Vacations (800) 872-7786, and America West Vacations (800) 356-6611 especially competitive and reasonably priced.

- *Off-the-rack travel*—Finding a hotel room at bargain basement prices is not unlike house hunting. The owners set an asking price, but they don't necessarily expect to get it. You should view the hotel's *rack* rate (industry lingo for *retail*) as just that: an asking price. But it should be the asking price for someone who doesn't know any better—certainly not for you. My sister Lori (you remember, the one who fell into the headboard) taught me the following rack-rate-lowering technique. Lori and her family were planning a trip to Walt Disney World and had their sights set on the Disney Yacht and Beach Club. However, when she called the hotel, Lori discovered that the rack rate was $250 a night, way out of her budget. Desperate, she pleaded, "Isn't there anything you can do? Have you got any special promotions going on?" Bingo! Without even knowing it, in her despair, Lori had uttered the right words!

  The hotel reservationist at 1-407-W-Disney told Lori to hold on while she checked. A few seconds later, the clerk reported the rack rate plunged miraculously from $250 per night to a special promotional rate of $150 per night. The moral of this story: hotels are rarely full, and an unused room is a loss to the hotel. The hotel would rather have a room occupied at a reduced rate than not occupied at all. Always ask for a better deal or special promotional rate when you're making reservations. Remember, though, that a central 800 reservations operator may not know about the lowest rates. It's worth making a long-distance call to the hotel directly to see what deals are available. If the hotel doesn't have any specials now, ask when the next promotions or value packages will be available. Again, you need to be persistent; if the reservationist doesn't know, ask to talk to someone in the marketing department. If you have flexibility in your plans, you may want to rearrange your vacation to take advantage of the promotion.

- *Timing is everything*—When you call to find out about special reduced rates, call during a slow period so the reservationists have time to answer your questions. I have found the best time to call is late at night, and the next best time is lunchtime. If the reservationist is not rushed, it's easier to form a sympathetic relationship with him/her, which certainly does not hurt your cause. (I'm still not quite sure how it happened, but when I arranged my birthday/anniversary/second honeymoon vacation at the Caribe Hilton in San Juan, I got so chummy with the reservationist that I gave her all the details about this extra-special vacation. When my husband and I arrived at the hotel, we were taken to a two-story, double-balconied penthouse with a separate sun room and double bathrooms, one of which was oversized and looked out over San Juan with floor-to-ceiling windows. All this was the same price as the standard room I had originally booked.)
- *No reservations*—Reduced rack rates are much harder to get on short notice. A word to the bargain wise: make your vacation plans as early as possible to snag discount room rates. Hotels like to plan ahead and fill up as many rooms as

possible. However, the hotel will try to accomodate you if you call in advance when the reservation computer screen still shows a large percentage of vacant rooms. Hotels don't want to lose your business, especially if the computer shows vacancies. Again, bargaining power is on your side, provided you call early.

- *Don't be shy*—Get your family the best possible room by preinspecting upon arrival. Remember house-hunting? You wouldn't buy a house without having a good look around, right? You will be living in your hotel room, albeit a short while, so why not be happy? Ask to see the room before you commit to it. Is the room too close to the ice machine? Excessive noise may keep you and the kids from a restful night. Only one queen-size bed for your family of four? But you distinctly requested two queen-size beds and a pullout couch. And what about that view? Overlooking the garbage dump behind the restaurant was not what you had in mind for your once-a-year fantasy escape from reality. In fact, you may want to look at several rooms before making a decision.
- *Don't get locked out*—Guard that confirmation number with your life. In fact, reconfirm one or two nights before you leave, and get the name of the hotel clerk who reconfirms your reservation. Call me paranoid, but there's nothing worse than hearing, "Oh, sorry, we don't have a reservation for Mr. Nitwit." Don't be one. The minute I get off the phone with my hot little confirmation number in hand, I immediately put it in my wallet, right behind the credit cards I will be using on the trip. (You may want to make a duplicate of the number and put it in one other safe place in the house, just in case. Or better yet, give a copy to your spouse or another adult who will be traveling with you.)
- *Don't get fooled again*—Just because a brochure or agent tells you that a room has an ocean view does not mean that your room is on, or anywhere near, the beach. At a rather upscale

hotel in California, we were disgruntled to find that the lovely ocean view from our beautiful room was visible, but it was necessary to cross a street to get to the ocean. When you travel with kids, having property directly on the beach where children can run right out is easiest, and you don't need to worry about them getting hit by a car. So ask ahead of time.

- *The meek may inherit the earth, but the outspoken will get the perks*—Smart shoppers sometimes need to become smart complainers to get a free night's stay, meal vouchers, or both. If you have been put out of your room by the hotel for any reason such as fire, electrical problems, flood, false alarms, whatever—if it interrupted your family's much-needed rest, not to mention threw the baby completely off schedule, and the little ones never got back to sleep—you're entitled to a refund for that lost night. Ask to speak to the manager and politely explain your plight. If he or she doesn't offer you compensation on the spot and instead gives you that, "What do you want me to do about it?" attitude, speak up. Say that you refuse to pay for the room because, after all, you were not able to use it for the purpose it was intended. I have found out that generally, if I persist, the managers usually give in (they don't like scenes). You should also receive some compensation if there are any other problems with your room from heating difficulties, unmade beds, no linen or towels, dirt, bugs, etc.
- *Checking it out (or in)*—Check-in and check-out times can cut into valuable vacation time. Check-in times usually range from 2 pm to 4 pm. You may want to call ahead and ask whether your room can be ready for an earlier arrival. This arrangement can help you in two ways. First, if you happen to arrive early, your room may actually be ready, or ready in a very short time (depending on whether someone else just checked out of the room). Second, how often have you had to wait an agonizingly long time for the hotel to make up your room?

This is not a great way to begin the vacation, especially with kids who are usually tired and cranky after a long car trip or plane ride. What about checking out? There's no need to rush and end the vacation any sooner than you want to. Simply call the front desk and ask if you can have an extended check-out. Most hotels can give you an extra one or two hours. I have never been turned down.

- *Market value*—Keep your eyes peeled for airline/supermarket promotions. These joint promotions have become popular. Major supermarket chains around the country offer several types of airline discounts of 30% to 50% off full fares. The next time you check out your groceries, check out customer service and see if the store has travel certificates that enable you to purchase discounted seats on selected major carriers. You will probably need to present register receipts (generally from $50 to $100 worth of purchases), buy a travel certificate (usually $5), and complete your roundtrip travel within a specified period of time.
- *Fasten your seat belt, it's going to be a bumped ride, you hope*—Are you interested in flying for free practically anywhere your airline goes? Sign in at the gate as a volunteer family willing to give up your seats in the event that the airline overbooked your scheduled flight. If you get called, the airline usually puts you on the next available flight and compensates you for your troubles with free passage anywhere along their routes. It's a good idea to mention this strategy to your family ahead of time, especially if your younger kids are likely to balk loudly at last-minute changes. In fact, you may want to play up this tactic as a way for your family to take an additional trip to someplace wonderful.
- *Join the club*—Pay attention to the airline's own in-flight publications, especially those for children. You may find additional

savings opportunities with coupons or club enrollments. For example, Delta's Fantastic Flyer Club (800 392-KIDS) offers a first-time enrollment promotion where one passenger purchases a ticket at a minimum price, then one child and two accompanying passengers receive 20% off the lowest fares. After your child is enrolled in the club, he or she receives quarterly issues of *Delta's Fantastic Flyer* magazine that, from time to time, mentions additional discount savings and coupons. One of our best airline buys came this way: our daughter's issue arrived with a $50 roundtrip travel coupon valid anywhere in the U.S. Together with the aforementioned 20% discounts for our tickets, we were sports and took little Missy to the land of Beverly Hills 90210 at rock-bottom prices.

Hotel Brokers

On any given night, on average, one-third of the 3.3 million hotel rooms in the United States are vacant, according to Entertainment Publications, Inc. Vacancy is not good for the hotel industry, but there's gold in them thar empty rooms for you! This is where the discount hotel brokers come in. These brokers operate much the same way airline consolidators work; the brokers buy up blocks of projected vacant rooms at select times of the year. The brokers can provide the rooms at 50% off the rack rate, but flexibility is the key to getting these discounts. Hotels may not be able to take your reservation during peak times or when trade shows and conventions come to town. After a hotel is booked to 80% capacity, it may not honor the broker's request. If possible, try to come up with alternate dates for your vacation getaways. I don't know about you, but I'm a much happier camper when the hotel is less crowded and service is better. The following sections describe several hotel brokers.

Express Reservations
(800) 356-1123

This discount airline and hotel broker offers the best of the best at 20% to 50% off rack rates at New York and Los Angeles properties. We were thrilled to see the very fabulous Loews Santa Monica Beach Hotel at incredible rates. (You may recognize this hotel as the backdrop to many a Beverly Hills 90210. Loews really does love kids; we've been there. More about this wonderful place later.) Other luxury hotels available through Express at up to 50% off rack are The Nikko-Beverly Hills (if you love dramatic bathrooms and deep-soak Japanese tubs, book this one, Dan-O!) and the Beverly Hills Hotel. In New York, your kids can re-enact scenes from the movie *Home Alone Two* when the family checks in at the Plaza Hotel at reduced prices.

Express also can help find you the lowest possible airfares. Use the price quote to compare to other airline quotes you get before booking.

HRN (Hotel Reservations Network)
(800) 964-6835 Mon.–Fri. 8–6 Central

This service can help you save from 40% to 65% on hotels in New York, Los Angeles, San Francisco, Chicago, Boston, Washington D.C., Orlando, New Orleans, San Diego, Anaheim, Miami, London, and Paris. HRN can book your family into some of the official hotels of the Disney Village such as Hilton, Grosvenor and Royal Plaza. Many of the Orlando properties allow kids not only to stay free but to eat free, too! If you book three nights or more, HRN gives you a bonus of 500 frequent flyer miles.

If you find that a city is completely sold out but you must have a room there, HRN claims it can find you one. However, in such cases, discounts may not be available.

HRN has no membership fees or costs; simply call the 800 number and book away.

Quikbook
(800) 789-9887

Specializing in smaller, boutique-type hotels, this broker offers discounts of 20% to 60% off the rack rate at some of the pricier hotels in the following cities: New York, Chicago, Atlanta, Boston, Washington D.C., Los Angeles, and San Francisco. Occasionally, you're getting an even better deal because breakfast is included in the room rate. You can choose from 50 hotels in the New York area. One of the best deals is the newly refurbished Omni Berkshire Place, where the average rack rate is about $325. Quikbook quoted us a discount price of $180 a night. The New York Palace has a listed rack rate of $300 to $320 per night; book the room with Quikbook and you pay $195. Or how about a standard room at the St. Moritz on Central Park South for $89 (limited promotion). Rack rates here start around $145. If you opt for the St. Moritz, treat your kids (and you too) to a Rumplemayers hot fudge sundae downstairs next to the main lobby. (This tip may be the most valuable advice in the whole book.)

Here's a sampling of some other nice hotels with great family deals available through Quikbook: The Hotel Nikko—Atlanta, The Westin Peachtree—Atlanta, Boston Park Plaza—Boston, The Colonnade Hotel—Boston, Intercontinental Hotel—Chicago, Hotel Sofitel (formerly Ma Maison Sofitel)—Beverly Hills, Beverly Prescott—Beverly Hills, Mondrian—West Hollywood, The Mark Hopkins—San Francisco, The Pan Pacific (very exclusive—each room has a personal butler)—San Francisco.

Quikbook does not charge membership fees. You pay nothing other than the cost of the room. Also, the sales staff is familiar with the individual properties. Explain what type of hotel you're looking for, and the staffers can suggest the right place for your taste and budget.

Room Exchange
(800) 846-7000 Mon.–Fri. 9–5 Eastern

Through this broker, you can select from 23,000 hotels in the United States, Caribbean, Europe, and the Far East at 25% to 65% off the rack rate. No costs or membership fees for this service. Thought you couldn't afford the posh Four Seasons? (The Four Seasons now caters to your child's needs and whims with their V.I.K. program—Very Important Kids—with special gifts, kid meals, activity programs, books, games, toys, strollers, kid robes, baby sitters, and lots more.) Try calling Room Exchange for a price quote, and you may be very surprised.

How about the exceptionally kid-friendly and very deluxe El Conquistador in Puerto Rico? We got an in-season price quote of $234 per night compared to the regular $369 (a 35% discount). Other better-quality, kid-friendly hotels to choose from at great reductions include the Hilton Hotels, Westin, Hyatt, and more.

All reservations must be prepaid with a credit card. However, you can cancel up to 48 hours in advance for U.S. properties and up to one week in advance for the Caribbean, Europe, and the Far East.

Airline Consolidators

These airline brokers are usually wholesalers who have contracts with major airline carriers and some charter companies, and buy blocks of airline seats in volume at discount prices and pass the savings on to customers. Remember, airlines are much like hotels; if they can predict a certain percentage of empty seats, they are glad to sell them at a discount price rather than risk losing the revenue entirely. Keep in mind, though, that you may have restrictions such as change fees ($50) and having to stay over a Saturday night. Also, you cannot always count on non-stop flights.

These consolidators often offer great deals, but you need to ask all the right questions—about price, restrictions, length of flight, etc. Check your local Sunday newspaper travel supplements for ads of low-fare ticket companies, which are generally the consolidators. You may want to check up on such shops with the Better Business Bureau before handing over your plastic. That way, you may be able to avoid problems with a newer, less established company.

Travel Byte

If you're flying with United Airlines and your child is a finicky eater like mine, you may want to reserve a McDonald's meal in the sky. Call at least 24 hours in advance of your flight and order a McDonald's kid meal, which comes with a toy and activity package to keep your child busy during the flight.

800–FLY–CHEAP

This group books most major airlines such as Northwest, Continental, Delta, TWA and others at competitive prices.

B.B. World Travel Inc.
Outside NYC: (800) 221-3158
Mon.–Fri. 9–5 Eastern time
NYC: (212) 797-1455

More a full-service travel agency than an airline consolidator, B.B. is listed here because of its unique service. The agents at B.B. can scan all the airline consolidators and airline promotions to compare airfares and find the lowest of the low airfares for you and your family. (Mention *The Smart Shopper's Guide* for extra-special attention.)

Cheap Tickets
(800) 377-1000 or (212) 570-1179

Although you may have difficulty getting through to this company, hang in there. You will be happily rewarded with some terrific savings. One of this company's Sunday newspaper ads featured round-trip airfare from New York to Miami at $145. (Some newspaper-ad fares may require a one-day advance purchase.) Cheap Tickets deals with major airlines including American, Delta, Continental, TWA, and Northwest and recommends that you book seven to 14 days in advance for the best fare quotes. The rock-bottom prices are usually available for flights on Tuesdays and Thursdays. Other restrictions apply, depending on the airline. For example, you may need to take a night flight or participate in a coach share (when two airlines actually share the flight). The bottom line: you'll save big bucks.

Travel Discounters
(800) 355-1065

Negotiated contracts with major carriers enable this consolidator to pass on $25 to $100 reductions on regular published airfares on Northwest, TWA, Continental, and on occasion, USAir and United. Book as far ahead as possible for the best selection of seats. Some restrictions on dates and time may apply. Travel Discounters also offers car rental discounts.

UniTravel
(800) 325-2222

This consolidator has been in business for over 27 years and is the most beneficial to last-minute travelers. If you have ever tried to make travel arrangements at the 11th hour, you know how expensive those tickets can be. UniTravel can cut those punishing fares by $200 to $300 per ticket. The company claims that it will match the lowest price. If you're traveling to Europe, especially during a peak European season such as autumn, UniTravel offers very competitive prices. Among the carriers the company uses are Delta, Northwest, TWA, Continental, USAir, American, United, KLM, Air France, British Airways, and Air India.

Low-Fare Carriers

Whatever you want to call them—low-fare, niche carriers, or upstarts—chances are you're not familiar with these airlines because they spend very little money advertising in order to keep their prices low. Some of these low-fare carriers have come a long way from the no-frills cattle-cars of a few years ago. In fact, Kiwi claims to have more legroom than scheduled carriers, superior food service, and fresh flowers in the bathrooms. You should investigate these airlines when you plan your next trip. In general, their prices are exceptionally low and drop even lower during special promotions. (Air South distributed free tickets for future flights during a special limited promotion—can't touch that!) Air routes are limited on these carriers. Also, prices tend to go up on *some* of these airlines when you buy closer to the flight date, so buy as far in advance as possible to get the best bargains.

The following table lists several low-fare airlines, their phone numbers, and destinations.

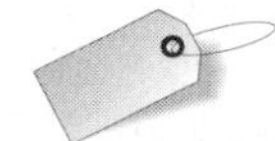

Bargain Byte

You thought Carnival just had cruise ships? Carnival Air (800-8AIR-FUN) is a full-service, low-fare air carrier that offers the cheapest airfare at all times with very few restrictions. The affordable first-class service includes four-course meals, ample legroom, and white glove service. How affordable is the first-class upgrade? Only $59 for one way on some northeast and Puerto Rico routes (if available) and $99 one way on the Florida to Los Angeles route. Take 25% off a $100 or more child's ticket when the child flies with a full-fare adult. (Don't forget to pre-order a kiddie meal and request a flight with a free movie aboard.) Carnival is also one of the few low-fare carriers that have a frequent flyer program for you, your kids, and your pets!

Finding Your Niche. . .Low-Fare Airlines

Airline	Phone #	Destinations
Air South	(800) AIR-SOUTH	Atlanta, Columbia, Raleigh, Jacksonville, Miami, Myrtle Beach, Newark, Charleston
Carnival	(800) 8AIRFUN	New York, Palm Beach, Miami, Fort Lauderdale, Orlando, Tampa, Newark, Islip (CT), Puerto Rico, Nassau, Los Angeles
Jet Train	(800) 359-4968	Newark, Orlando, Pittsburgh
Jet Express	(800) 386-2786	Boston, Cleveland, Detroit, New York, Myrtle Beach, Newark, Chicago, Philadelphia, Atlanta, Mobile

continues

Kiwi International	(800) 538-5494	Newark, Atlanta, Bermuda, Chicago Midway, Las Vegas, Orlando, West Palm Beach, Tampa
Midway	(800) 446-4392	Providence, Boston, Hartford, Newark, Washington, D.C., Norfolk, Las Vegas, Orlando, Tampa, West Palm Beach, Cancun, Asheville, Spartanburg, Hilton Head, Myrtle Beach, Charleston
Southwest Airlines	(800) 435-9792	Baltimore, Columbus, Omaha, Portland, Spokane, Tampa, Fort Lauderdale, Orlando, Dallas, Las Vegas, New Orleans, San Diego, Austin, etc.
Sun Jet	(800) 478-6538	Newark, Fort Lauderdale, Orlando, St. Petersburg, Dallas, Long Beach (CA), Los Angeles
Tower Air	(800) 34-TOWER	New York, Miami, San Juan, Los Angeles, San Francisco, Paris, Amsterdam, Tel Aviv, New Delhi, Bombay (Athens, Rome, Milan chartered)
Western Pacific	(800) 930-3030	San Jose, Nashville, Colorado Springs, Dallas, Houston, Las Vegas, Los Angeles, Oklahoma City, Phoenix, San Diego, etc.

Bargain Byte

Most of these travel clubs issue a plastic, charge-type membership card. You may need to register your identification number to activate the card. Register immediately then put the card in your wallet with the rest of your credit cards. You need to present the card to all merchants, restaurants, and hotel establishments to qualify for discounts.

Join a Travel Club, Clip a Coupon

Even if you're not an inveterate coupon-clipper, it's not too late to start. Several travel discounters operate much like a featured coupon club. You pay a membership fee and receive a book listing the discounts. To take advantage of the discounts, you show a membership card or present a coupon. Here's a rundown of the most popular travel discount clubs:

Dine-A-Mate
(800) 660-1134

Annual fee $20–$30. You can purchase individual city/area premium books that feature local restaurants where you can "buy one (entree), get one free." Dine-A-Mate also publishes a National Travel and Hotel Directory that lists over 2,500 hotels and resorts in the U.S. and Canada and 1,500 accommodations throughout Europe, Australia, China, the Caribbean, South America, and Mexico where you can get 50% off the rack rate. This directory also has airfare coupons, car rental discounts, tourist attraction and theme park admission reductions, value packages, and cruise line discounts. There are individual publications for cities in Arizona, Alabama, California, Connecticut, Florida, Georgia, Kansas, Kentucky, Massachusetts, Nebraska, New Jersey, North Carolina, New York, Oregon, Pennsylvania, South Carolina, Texas, and Washington. (Other cities are expected to be added; call for more information.)

Entertainment Publications Inc.
(800) 445-4137
(800) 374-4464

This company publishes more than 100 directories to cities and countries ($28 to $48) that feature hotel, restaurant, and other discounts. The National Hotel & Dining Directory ($42.95) includes listings for discounts of up to 50% at more than 3,500 hotels worldwide, along with 20% off the total bill for up to six people dining together at selected restaurants. If a hotel listed in the directory is running a special promotional rate that matches or beats Entertainment's discount, you receive a 10% discount below the promotional rate.

Entertainment also has discount air coupons (the '96 edition featured significant discounts on American Airlines and Continental), rental car reductions, and savings coupons to local and national attractions and theme parks including Sea World, Busch Gardens, Sesame Place, and Six Flags.

IGT (In Good Taste)
(800) 992-TRAV

Annual fee $48. IGT gives you 25% discounts in hotels, resorts, and restaurants included in the company directory. Updated directories and newsletters with additions and deletions are sent monthly. Domestic lodging and accommodations are limited here to Colorado, Florida, Nevada, New York, Pennsylvania, Texas, New Orleans, Caribbean, and nationwide Howard Johnsons.

ITC-50
(800) 342-0558

Annual fee $36–$79. This International Travel Card (the 50 stands for, what else, 50% off) gets you 50% off all hotels listed in the directory. A smaller dining directory offers discounts on meals. If you're a member of Amoco or Sears Motor Club, you should receive special ITC-50 offers in the mail; if you haven't, call your motor club and ask for them.

Quest
(800) 742-3543

Annual fee $99. You get 50% off the rack rate at hotels listed in the Quest directory. Again, if a weekend or other promotional rate is the same or lower than the Quest rate, you receive a 10% reduction off the promo rate. Quest members also can take 25% off the total restaurant bill at all participating restaurants. Airfare coupons in the guide offered $35 to $100 off on Northwest and $25 to $50 off on Delta Dream Vacations to Walt Disney World. Other hotels available through this program include the Omni Royal Orleans (New Orleans), Stouffer Wailea Beach Resort (Hawaii), and Radisson Normandie (San Juan, Puerto Rico).

Another unique feature is Quest's Condo Program. If you're more comfortable staying in a furnished condo with several bedrooms and a kitchen, you can save 50% or more at resort condos in North America including Scottsdale, Palm Springs, Florida Keys, Puerto Vallarta, Hawaii, Las Vegas, Hilton Head, Aruba, St. Maarten, Barbados, Grand Bahama, Mexico, and Lake Tahoe.

Transmedia
(800) 422-5090

Annual fee $50. Better known as a discount dining club offering 25% off at 6,000 restaurants around the world including the U.S., United Kingdom, and Australia, Transmedia now offers hotel discounts. You can save up to 25% off rooms at participating hotels. The frequent flyer program gives you 10 frequent flyer miles for each dollar spent with Transmedia on United and Continental.

Local Travel Guides and Coupon Premiums

Convention and visitor's bureaus in major cities generally provide travel booklets that consist of maps, calendars of events, vacation planners, hotel accommodations, local tourist attractions, dining information, etc. Coupons for discounts (worth from $200 to $2,500!) on everything from hotels to restaurants to tourist attraction admissions are often included. When you're traveling around the country, call local information for the convention and visitor's bureau number. Then request the local guide book and coupon packet. Coupon books are subject to availability and expiration dates. Here's a rundown of some of the best of these local discount books:

- Orlando Magicard (800) 645-4873. This is an actual plastic charge-type card; it's a must if you're going to Disney World.
- Kissimee/St. Cloud Vacation Guide (Walt Disney World Area) (800) 831-1844
- Islamorada, Florida (The Keys) (800) FAB-KEYS. This book has water activity and dive excursion discounts in addition to hotel and dining offers.

- Key Largo, Florida (The Keys) (800) 822-1088
- Palm Beach, Florida (407) 471-3995. These coupon books are available only from April through December.
- Pennsylvania (800) VISIT-PA
- Philadelphia, Pennsylvania (800) 770-5886. Philadelphia Loves Visa value book offers discounts and freebies for some 350 attractions including the Philadelphia Orchestra. All transactions must be made with a Visa card.
- Missouri Fun Money (800) 877-1234
- Virginia Beach (800) 446-8038
- New Orleans Good Times Guide (800) 632-3116
- San Diego Value Pack (619) 236-1212
- Boston (800) 888-5515. Request the Kids Love Boston Package.
- Ohio (800) BUCKEYE. Don't forget to visit the Rock 'n' Roll Hall of Fame!
- Nevada Bonus Book (800) NEVADA-8
- Vermont (800) 24-STOWE. Ask for both the free vacation planner and the coupon book.

Affordable Luxury Accommodations for You and the Kids

The following list contains some of the leading, affordable, child-friendly properties in the United States and Caribbean that we know about or have visited. Of course, we haven't been everywhere, so some terrific hotels and resorts may not be included. However, we would be glad to research any particular facilities you're interested in and possibly include them in the next edition of *The Smart*

Shopper's Guide. Drop us a line (P.O. Box 797, Forest Hills, NY 11375) and let us know what you want to know.

Keep in mind these few pointers on taking advantage of money-saving deals and special children's programs:

""

Savvy and Silly Celebrity Travel Tips from...
Sally Jessy Raphael

"Because of the nature of broadcasting, one has to live at times like a gypsy. There are just so many jobs in any one town. When our adopted son J.J. was three years old, my husband Karl and I packed up and moved from Florida to Hartford, CT. To get there cheaply, we drove. We had a lot of miles to cover each day, so I'd wash J.J.'s clothes in the motel at night. They were usually not dry in the morning, so we'd tie them to the antenna of the car. And you should see the looks we got!"

""

- Check out the aforementioned hotel consolidators and hotel directories and see if they represent the hotel or hotel chain you're interested in (the hotel reservationist can tell you which consolidators and directories the hotel uses). If the properties don't work with discounters, ask about the lowest, off-season, mid-week, weekend prices and any additional promotional rates.
- Find out how child-friendly the hotel is. Ask what programs are offered and press for details about the activities, supervision, age limits, babysitting services, and any special children's menus.
- Don't forget to ask about any "kids stay free and eat free" promotions.

Here are details on some great family-friendly hotels:

The Ritz Carlton
Palm Beach, Naples, Cancun, Rancho Mirage
(800) 241-3333

Putting on the Ritz—with kids! If you're going to vacation, do it right. From the moment you pull up to a Ritz Carlton, it's upperclass all the way. Don't expect flashy, contemporary decor; tasteful and traditional with an abundance of fresh floral arrangements and deep mahogany is the Ritz style. Years ago, you probably would never have considered taking the kids to such an exclusive property. Well, they've come a long way, baby! In fact, the Ritz properties welcome babies, kids, and teens with the Ritz Kids programs at select Ritz Carlton resorts.

For the past several years, Ritz properties in Palm Beach, Cancun, Rancho Mirage (near Palm Springs), and Naples have lowered their off-season, summer rates to the discount tune of \$129–\$134 per night.

(Compare this with the in-season rates at Palm Beach: $325–$650 per night!) And there's no skimping on the rooms. We tried the summer special at the Palm Beach location and had a spacious room with a generous-sized balcony overlooking the Atlantic ocean. My daughter was in heaven with the capacious bathroom complete with private commode and wall phone, princess-like toiletries, and sumptuous appointments like crystal faucets, plush terry towels, robes, and marble tile.

During the day, kids can enjoy seashell hunts, seashell arts and crafts, scavenger hunts through the Ritz Carlton's botanical gardens, swimming, tennis, and more. In the evening, the Ritz supper club (an additional $20) entertained the kids with dinner and a movie while parents relaxed and enjoyed a meal in peace. (Wow you're a great parent, you took your kids to the Ritz! Now you deserve a break, and I don't mean McDonald's!) Your child also can pick from a children's menu and have room service. (If you go to the Ritz in Palm Beach and your child is a fan of Playmobil toys, don't forget to visit the Playmobil Park in Palm Beach Gardens—see Chapter 4 for details.)

The Boca Raton Resort & Club
(800) 327-0101

The exquisite Boca Raton Resort & Club offers a "Best of Boca Package" value deal including a deluxe room, breakfast, and dinner daily for the adults (separate kid's menu available), and specialized children's programs. Over the past few summers, from May 24 to September 30, the rates have ranged from $202–$210 per night.

The newly expanded children's program consists of Boca Tots (ages 3–5), Boca Bunch (ages 6–10), Boca Sport (11–13), and Boca Raton 33432 (ages 14–17). *Parents* magazine has rated the Boca Raton Resort as one of its top 10 family-tested destinations. If your child needs swimming instruction, you can look into Rob McKay's Lifestyle Swim School where children ages 8 months through 13 are taught swimming and water safety. Other activities for families to enjoy together include sun and fun cruises, old-fashioned family ice-cream Sundays, movies, and bingo. The camp programs offer activities including Boca Birds Scavenger Hunt, edible art and themed dinner parties, stunt kite flying, banana boat rides (hold on tight!), snorkeling, Techno-Funk and Other Junk dance parties, and my personal favorite, the turtle walk—depending on mother nature's whims, counselors show kids where turtles have laid eggs on the beach and explain the significance of preserving endangered wildlife.

Clubs International
(800) 777-1250 in the U.S. and Canada
(212) 251-1709 in New York State

Here are three properties that make visiting the Caribbean fun, easy, and affordable for families. The latest deal offers summer rates all year 'round! Start with Club St. Lucia (call American Airlines or BWIA to get there), where a double-share, standard room for $200 (ceiling fan) or $226 (air-conditioned) entitles a family of three (two adults, one child) to daily breakfast, lunch, dinner, snacks, all beverages (including alcohol for adults) and all sports and recreational activities. That's pretty good for an all-inclusive price. The resort boasts two sandy beaches, swimming pools, tropical gardens, exercise room, discotheque, shopping arcade, racquet club, and nine-hole golf course. The all-inclusive sister property, Club Antigua, offers slightly less expensive rooms. You can get the same deal for $187 (double room minimum with ceiling fan) or $200 (double room with air conditioning). Family rooms are available for a slightly higher price and feature a bedroom with king-size bed, separate living room with couch-bed that sleeps two additional adults or children, plus patio area.

The kids' programs are free; the 4- to 12-year-olds will be busy most of the day with videos, cartoons, face-painting, T-shirt designing, games, field trips, and cooking classes utilizing ingredients indigenous to the island. Teen programs are also available.

If you would rather set up housekeeping in the Caribbean, you may want to try the Jolly Harbour Marina Club condos in Antigua. These modern two-bedroom condos start at $80 per night and one child under 12 can stay free.

All condos have a waterfront patio view and private mooring space for your yacht! A fully equipped kitchen enables you to prepare meals in the room. Separate living rooms are also fully furnished, and you have your choice of a one- or two-bathroom unit. All guests have free access to the large, freshwater swimming pool located in the sports complex. Shops, restaurants, salons, boat chartering services, bicycle rentals, and dive center are also available within the Jolly Harbour Marina. You can even rent a motorized golf cart for fun and easy local transportation. Kids love this!

Palm Springs Marquis Crown Plaza Resort & Suites
150 South Indian Canyon Drive
Palm Springs, CA 92262
(800) 223-1050

If you want to feel like a celebrity, follow the stars to Palm Springs. This charming, deluxe resort hotel lowers its summer rates to an unbelievable $68 per night for a standard but spacious room. (Kids 12 and under stay free.) For a splurge, a mountain-view, one-bedroom suite for a family of four, complete with kitchen, fireplace, sunken tub, and wet bar, starts at $87 per night. The resort also offers a kids-eat-free program, which allows kids under 12 to receive one complimentary breakfast or dinner from the children's menu for each adult entree ordered in the Garden Court Restaurant.

Kamp Wannakombak (cute?) operates daily at the hotel from 10am–9pm. The program has plenty of activities including pool fun, parties, games, crafts, ping pong, videos, storytelling, and snacks.

You can buy discount tickets at the hotel for nearby entertainment at the Palm Springs Aerial Tramway, local movies, and the Oasis Water Park. Or you can try a day hike in nearby Indian Canyons or an excursion to the Living Desert Wildlife and Botanical park. Palm Springs on a budget, who'd have thunk it?

Walt Disney World Swan Hotel
1200 Epcot Resort Blvd.
Lake Buena Vista, FL 32830
(800) 248-SWAN

This one's a first-class compromise for those adults who don't cherish the prospect of going to Disney World in the first place. Your kids enjoy the thrill of staying at Disney World (and you can't get much more centrally located than this place) while you relax at a superior property. The Swan Hotel is an exquisite, four-diamond luxury resort that makes you forget you're in the middle of the land of the Disneys. If you ask for the lowest possible rate, and if any special promotions are happening, you probably can knock off at least $100 from the rack rate. During the summer of 1996, the Swan's regular rack rate of $280 dropped to $175 for a standard room. Florida residents may get a discount ranging from $139–$145 (per night), just to give you an idea of pricing. Value packages with four-day Disney park passes are also available.

The hotel itself is rather unique in appearance with 42-foot swans perched rooftop, three acres of grotto swimming pool complete with waterfalls and a kid-friendly water slide. (Lifeguards were extremely watchful and solicitous of kids coming off the slide; however, I recommend at least one parent keep an extra eye on the kids because it gets very crowded.) The Swan Hotel has a beachfront (no swimming here, though), rental watercraft, tennis center, Camp Swan, and video game room. Choose from four unique dining facilities including a stunning Japanese restaurant, sushi bar (karaoke, of course!) and hotel bakery (partially glass-enclosed so you can watch the baking), where kids can try their hand at the culinary arts (and you can try the carrot cake). The lobby coffee and pastry bar is a great way to unwind after a hectic day at the parks (don't forget that carrot cake).

Access to the Disney parks couldn't be easier; you can walk, board a tram to Epcot, hop a bus to the Magic Kingdom, or cruise the ferry from the resort's boat dock to Disney MGM studios. Hi-ho!

Cheeca Lodge, Islamorada, Florida
P.O. Box 527
Islamorada, FL 33036
(mile marker 82)
(800) 327-2888

Only 75 miles from Miami, this casually elegant, four-diamond resort has been steadily gaining in popularity with Florida families in the know. Located amidst the "sport-fishing capital of the world," this resort offers an award-winning, ecologically oriented camp for children and a first-class getaway for adults. Celebrities and U.S. presidents alike have fished and vacationed here; in the Light Tackle Lounge, you may see a letter of thanks from *Seinfeld* co-star Jason Alexander who stayed here.

The hotel offers day and night dive trips, two swimming pools, 1,100-foot beach, separate beach-lined lagoon, nine-hole golf course, tennis, and sport-fishing (bone-fishing lures sports enthusiasts to this resort). If you fish out on the reef where grouper and snapper are abundant, the Cheeca chefs will be glad to prepare the catch for your evening dinner. Cheeca Lodge's main restaurant, The Atlantic Edge, serves five-star meals. (See Chapter 5 for more about this wonderful eatery.)

Now what price for all this glory? Normally, such divinity does not go cheap. In season, room rates range from $300 to $650; however, families on a budget can take advantage of the Purple Isle Dive Package available in the off-season from the end of April to mid-December, where a room goes for $119 per night! The package entitles you to the room, a 10% discount on purchases in the dive center, and 50% off Camp Cheeca (regularly $26 daily). All packages are subject to availability. To get in on this great deal, flexibility of dates is key to your going to the Keys, in style.

Jekyll Island Club Hotel, Jekyll Island, Georgia
371 Riverview Drive
Jekyll Island, GA 31527
(912) 635-2600

Named one of the top 50 resorts in the continental U.S. by *Conde Nast Traveler*, this Victorian landmark hotel was originally a hunting retreat for J.P. Morgan, William Rockefeller, and friends at the turn of the century. You fly into Jacksonville and then pick up the hotel van. Your kids will love seeing turkeys, waterfowl, and deer running wild on this barrier island off the coast of Georgia. Or the kids can join Club Juniors where they can swim in the nearly Olympic-size pool, play tennis or lawn sports, go crabbing on the beach, or fly kites, to name just a few activities. Most kids can't wait for Friday mornings when *That's Entertainment* brings musicians, magicians, clowns, puppeteers, nature ladies, and even snake handlers to perform for the kids.

Nearby are 22 miles of flat bicycle paths, a water park, guided nature walks, fishing opportunities, and the hotel's old-fashioned beach Pavillion and veranda where you can enjoy snacks while gazing at the ocean.

The columned, grand dining room is headed up by chef Bruce Ford, a graduate of the Culinary Institute of America in Hyde Park, New York. The continental American cuisine includes traditional southern dishes as well as more unusual fare from blackened Cajun-style amberjack to Georgia white shrimp. Café Solterra offers more casual meals including sandwiches, pizza, and pastries like chocolate decadence and blackberry bakewell.

During the summer, you can escape to this National Historic Landmark, four-star, four-diamond resort for a mere $345 for a three-night package, $436 for a four-night package, or $495 for a five-night package. Included in the package price are overnight accommodations, children's program, tennis, and use of resort amenities. Don't forget to sample the resort's afternoon tea in the Riverview Room.

Rocking Horse Ranch, Highland, New York
Highland, NY 12528
(800) 647-2624

I wouldn't *steer* you wrong—it's not the Ritz Carlton (how many dude ranches are?), but kids do love this place only $1\frac{1}{2}$ hours from New York City. The ranch has won raves in several family magazines, and it has implemented bargain rates during select times of the year.

Call the ranch to be put on the mailing list. Then you get advance notice of the 10% to 50% off regular rate dates. (Discount dates and rates vary from year to year.) Rates here are all-inclusive covering lodging, meals, seasonal sports, horseback riding, day camp, use of the three heated pools (one indoor), and evening entertainment. For example, a regular six-day, five-night package for a family of four normally runs from $1,270 to $1,370; with the maximum discount, the tab comes to $653 to $685! (Book early to avoid the stampede.)

I'm not horsing around when I tell you that this place has an endless array of activities from water skiing, snow skiing, paddle boats, petting zoo, banana boats, lake ice-skating, tobogganing, hay rides, sleigh rides, tennis, archery, miniature golf, fishing, basketball, riflery, pizza and ice cream parties, and on and on. For ultimate worrywarts like myself, you can select from hundreds of safety helmets if you and the kids are going riding. Any "nay" sayers? Remember to watch your step!

The Village at Smuggler's Notch
Smuggler's Notch, VT 05464
(800) 451-8752 U.S. and Canada

How would you like a money-back guarantee if you're not completely satisfied with the program portion of your vacation? Smuggler's Notch is so confident about the quality of the resort's activity offerings that it puts forth this promise. (If you're wondering whether the resort has ever had to provide a refund, it has only a few times, mostly related to sickness.)

Guarantee aside, let's take a look at what many people consider this to be the ideal family resort. This is the first vacation my family ever took where the fun began before we arrived. It was an adventure driving up the spectacular, but steep, Vermont mountains and winding around sharp turns (it's a good idea to go slow and honk when you turn because the road narrows) to get to the Notch. This method seems to be the path of choice when visiting Smuggler's during the warmer months (you could never manage this with snow and ice on the roads). Be prepared for screams and squeals from the kids on this somewhat treacherous journey. Don't forget to stop at the caves (they have ice during the summer, and peregrine falcons fly above the cliffs), which was a final stop of the Underground Railroad around Civil War time and a famous hiding point for alcohol smugglers (hence the resort's name) from Canada during prohibition.

After you are safely inside Smuggler's Village (I don't think they've lost anyone yet on the ride up), you probably won't know where to begin. Start with a good look at the gorgeous view in front of you. Smuggler's is surrounded on three sides by the breathtaking Vermont Green Mountains.

If you have little ones, you may want to check out the fully certified and very impressive Alice's Wonderland Child Care Center. This state-of-the-art facility is designed specifically for the needs of infants, toddlers, and small children. It has crib rooms, fish tanks, hands-on sand and water tables, videos, six-foot teddy bears, storytelling, and more. Of course, the older kids will be jumping into their swimsuits and attacking the 30-foot-high Giant Rapids River Ride & Waterslides. Other exciting summertime activities include hiking, mountain biking, fishing, canoeing (try the Sunset Beaver Watch), llama treks, tennis, golf, swimming, paddle boats, and more. In the colder months, this place turns into a winter wonderland. At the snowmaking center, you can watch snow being made via pumps, pipes, computers, and compressors! There's an abundance of ski trails of every level. Kids can join the ski and snowboard camp where they're occupied all day with lessons, lunch, and activities.

All this great action doesn't come cheap. (Expect extra charges for the day camps and programs.) However, there are ways to bring down costs significantly. First, try to arrange a share with another family and reserve one of the larger-size (up to five bedrooms) luxury condos and patio. This arrangement can cut your costs in half. In June, the special value month, prices drop about 40%. To save on food, you may want to venture into the adjoining towns and find out where the locals eat. Call the number listed earlier for comprehensive brochures and vacation planners. If you plan on taking the Ben & Jerry's ice cream factory tour just down the mountain from Smuggler's in Stowe (and you really should), call ahead and reserve a space; otherwise you may need to wait up to two hours during the peak summer season.

Loews Hotels

(800) 23-LOEWS

The luxurious Loews hotels and resorts have launched a Loews Loves Kids program that has numerous benefits: special discounts on a second adjoining room; children under 18 stay free when sharing a room with parents; children's menus in restaurants and through room service; complimentary use of roll-away beds and cribs; child-proof kits for children under four; and kid-oriented concierge services.

Each property has individual programs that complement the surroundings and facilities. One of the most exciting hotels in the chain is the Loews Santa Monica Beach Hotel. The Splash Club, featured during summer months, offers T-shirt making, puppets, kite-flying, volleyball, treasure hunts in the pool, sandcastle-building contests, relay races, and more. You definitely want to rent some roller blades or bikes next to the hotel and head down the beach path toward the Santa Monica Pier for some quintessential California action. In the evening, don't be surprised if there's a knock at the door from room service treating everyone to milk and the most delectable chocolate chip cookies for bedtime (see Chapter 5 for the recipes). The staff even brings up age-appropriate bedtime stories for the kids.

Loews lowers rates significantly during the summer months, even offering 50% off second room rates. Remember to check with the aforementioned discount travel networks to explore additional savings at these very lovely and very kid-friendly properties.

Hilton Hotels Vacation Stations

(800) HILTONS

Save up to 40% in conjunction with Hilton Hotels' ongoing bounceback program. You will find free Hilton Vacation Stations in 80 Hilton properties throughout the U.S. Hilton's program for families traveling with children includes welcome gifts upon registration and supervised activity programs at select properties. The stations are open seven days a week and provide kids with a comprehensive game-lending library including most toys from Hasbro, Kenner, Milton Bradley, and Playskool. From board games to hand-held video games, you can find something for every child's taste. Of course, kid menus are always available in restaurants and through room service. Free continental breakfasts are available at select hotels and resorts; inquire when reserving. If your kids are really adventurous, look into Camp Coyote at the Pointe Hilton Resort at Squaw Peak, Arizona, where the kids can actually pan for gold.

The Peaks at Telluride, Colorado

136 Country Club Drive
Telluride, CO 81435
(800) 789-2220

Why should grown-ups have all the fun and relaxation opportunities? This four-diamond resort has cleverly created a supervised KidSpa program for the ultimate in child-pampering. Through KidSpa, children of all ages are invited to participate in yoga classes that integrate relaxation techniques, energetic hikes, swimming (kids adore the water slide that connects an indoor lap pool to a lower-level indoor/outdoor pool), skiing and snowboarding lessons, spa-cuisine cooking instruction, and of course, panning for gold in nearby streams. (Telluride is famous for its prolific gold strikes that brought more than $16 million in gold and silver between 1905 and 1911.)

The Peaks is a truly exquisite resort with breathtaking views of Colorado's San Juan Mountain Range. Readers of *Conde Nast Traveler* voted the 42,000 square-foot Spa as one of the top 10 in the U.S. Parents can indulge in four treatments that make use of local plant life such as alpine strawberries, local pine, and herbal essences that rejuvenate, relax, and assist in adjusting to Telluride's high altitude.

Rates can climb as steep as a mountain range here, but with early-season ski packages and off-season rates, you can save almost 50% off the in-season prices, making this exceptional facility affordable for families. Figure around $220 a day in contrast with high-season's $405 per day. Charges for the KidSpa program begin at around $40 for a full day or $25 for a half day.

Plantation Inn at Ocho Rios, Jamaica, West Indies

(800) 752-6824

If you're at all familiar with this world-class resort, voted one of the "best places to stay in the world" according to *Conde Nast Traveler's* Gold List, you're probably wondering how it made the list. (You may recall that this resort was the honeymoon destination of Alec Baldwin and Meg Ryan in *Prelude to a Kiss.*) Until recently, few kids under age 12 ever stayed here. However, now that the Plantation has hopped on the luxury resort child-friendly bandwagon, kids of all ages can enjoy a very special holiday.

If your child appreciates warm, azure waters, quiet beaches, tropical gardens, lush surroundings, culinary delights, and individually tailored activity programs such as stone painting, nature walks, and reggae dance classes, this resort may indeed be for you. Windsurfing, snorkeling, glass-bottom boat rides, and sunfish sailboats are also available on the beach at no extra charge.

Travel in the off-season from mid-March to mid-December, and you can reel this one in for around $130 a night for a superior room; the two-bedroom penthouse suite goes for about $460. In-season rates range from around $195 to $715. Quite a savings! All rooms have balconies, ocean views, and beautiful furnishings in polished mahogany.

The Westin La Paloma, Tucson, Arizona
3800 East Sunrise Drive
Tucson, AZ 85718
(800) 876-3683

This four-star/four-diamond resort nestled in the foothills north of Tucson may be one of the most kid-friendly and kid-ready of them all. During the value season, kids 12 and under eat and stay free (kids 13–18 stay free only if sharing a room with parents). Plus, you can save over 50% on the regular rack rates.

From the moment you register, your children are treated royally. They're welcomed with a free, age-appropriate gift, and you receive a child safety kit including outlet covers, child ID bracelets, bandages, a night light, safety tips for vacationing in a desert environment, and snake venom antidotes (just kidding, but not a bad idea). Child-size robes are also provided for your kids to use during their stay. Based upon need, your room can be outfitted with crib, bed railing, highchair, and even potty seats. Plus the mini bar is well-stocked with snacks and refreshments for all whipper-snappers. (Jogging strollers are free for the asking while vacationing here.)

The Westin La Paloma makes dining with kids easy by offering preferred family dining reservations and Express Meal Service.

The Westin Kids Club is available for children 6 months to 12 years in the children's lounge. The program offers supervised activities including storytelling, Nintendo, arts 'n' crafts, movies, and an outdoor play yard. Junior Tennis Camp (with swim breaks) and Family Golf Clinic are also available at a nominal charge. But the most outstanding feature for most kids is the hotel's 177-foot waterslide in the main, free-form pool.

For mom and dad, you should know that this luxury resort features 27 holes of Jack Nicklaus Signature golf, championship tennis, health center, pool with swim-up bar, and five restaurants.

Boston Park Plaza Hotel
64 Arlington St.
Boston, MA 02076
(800) 899-2076

The very elegant Boston Park Plaza has an outstanding Cub Club family value package at approximately $149 a night in first-class accommodations. Your family can stretch out in a very spacious child-proof room with two double beds and two baths. (Make sure to request rooms with full-size bathtubs, not just showers!) The package also includes valet parking and a coupon book valued at $1,000, offering discounts to great attractions all over New England such as the Plymouth Plantation, Children's Museums, Swan Boat Rides, Whale Watch, Trolley Tours, Yesteryear's Doll Museum, Old Stourbridge Village, Vermont's Sugarbush Resort, and the breathtakingly beautiful Trapp Family Lodge (the *Sound of Music* family) in Stowe, Vermont.

The Boston Park Plaza Hotel has hosted a number of sitting presidents since it was built in 1927, including Franklin Delano Roosevelt, Harry Truman, Richard Nixon, and John F. Kennedy. In fact, President Clinton seems to stay exclusively at the Boston Park Plaza when visiting Boston. And what has President Clinton ordered up from room service during each of his stays? Chicken fajitas—a Mexican dish of sauteed vegetables, tortillas, guacamole, and sour cream. And he likes to wash them down with lots of caffeine—free Diet Coke!

But don't worry, the hotel staff takes great pains to avoid inconveniencing other guests when celebrities are present. For example, when pop singer Elton John was staying at the hotel's Presidential suite, a hotel security officer had to ask him to refrain from late-night piano playing.

The FAO Schwartz-outfitted video/game play den and children's story hour (complete with milk and cookies) can keep the kids busy when you take a touring break. (Don't forget to pay homage, but not much money, to the original Filene's Basement for spectacular clothes bargains for the whole family. I once picked up a DKNY dress for my daughter at Filene's for 75% off the retail price.)

One of the six restaurants featured at the hotel is none other than the famous and mouth-watering Legal Seafood. Bring on the lobsters!

The Phoenician, Scottsdale, Arizona
6000 East Camelback Road
Scottsdale, AZ 85251
(800) 888-8234 or (602) 941-8200

For the ultimate in luxury resorts, The Phoenician is a combination Mobil five-star hotel, world-class health spa (The Center for Well-Being), and fine art museum with a collection of antiques and art valued at $1.7 million. This architecturally rich and exquisite property spreads out on 130 acres at the base of Camelback Mountain. So what do kids have to do with it? Plenty. The renowned Funicians (what else?) Club for children features a comprehensive and thoughtful program highlighting a different theme (Desert Discovery Day, Earth Watch Day, Wild West Day, Easy Etiquette Day) and coordinating activities each day. Children age five through adolescent can choose from swimming (seven heated pools, whirlpool, and 165-foot water slide), biking, croquet, chess, computers, hiking, volleyball, Medicine Wheel Ceremony, desert adventures, ice-cream socials, pizza parties, duck and fish feeding, Kachina art, recyclable crafts, golf, tennis, Nintendo, movies, hoola-hoops, cactus garden tours, afternoon tea,
family cookouts, and more.

During summer months, The Phoenician rates plummet to around $155 per night with up to two children 17 and under staying free in the parent's room. In-season rates range $330–$465 for commensurate accommodations.

Los Abrigados, Sedona, Arizona
160 Portal Lane
Sedona, AZ 86336
(800) 521-3131 or (602) 282-1777

If you're planning a trip to the Grand Canyon and feel like doing it in grand style, consider this ultimate vacation destination, which is reputed to be one of the finest resorts in Arizona. Los Abrigados has served as a getaway retreat and on-location home for many celebrities including Lloyd and Beau Bridges, Donald Sutherland,

Amy Irving, Lily Tomlin, Ann Miller, and Don Ameche to name a few. And no wonder, with a 10,000-square-foot world-class health spa on a creekside location surrounded by towering red rock formations. Invigorating activities run the gamut from jogging trails, hot air ballooning, horseback riding, tennis, fishing, jeep tours, golf, river rafting, highly acclaimed gourmet/casual dining, and an innovative children's Fun Club program. This resort appears to have something for everyone, including the most seasoned traveler.

Now for the music to your pocketbook. If you call and request (this is imperative) the "Bed & Breakfast" special, available Sunday through Thursday, you can book a full suite including breakfasts for $95 per night and $10 per child. The regular rate for this deal is $210 per night. The all-day rate for the kids Fun Club is $25 (including lunch and snack) or $15 for the half-day program.

Los Abrigados has become famous in recent years for its holiday-time Red Rock Fantasy, which begins the Wednesday prior to Thanksgiving and continues through January 11. This stunning light display features over 1 million holiday lights glittering throughout the property in various themed displays from "Under the Sea" to more traditional visuals.

Don't forget to take the kids over to nearby Slide Rock Park to try the natural-rock water slide during the summer.

Historic Strasburg Inn, Strasburg, Pennsylvania

One Historic Drive
Strasburg, PA 17579
(717) 687-7691

Kids and parents alike get a kick out of exploring the Amish country in Lancaster, Pennsylvania, still popular after all these years. There's too much to do, and everything is reasonably priced, if not downright cheap. But where to stay? If you want to stay with the flavor of the trip in delightful colonial accommodations, then the Strasburg Inn on 58 lush, sprawling acres is the perfect choice.

Smack dab in the middle of everything, (you can actually hear the steam whistle from the Strasburg Railroad), this lovely resort welcomes children (the Inn has no formal kids program, but trust me, you don't need it on this trip) and even has bike rentals on the property for you and the kids. The resort has a heated outdoor swimming pool, two restaurants (the formal George Washington House and the casual By George Tavern), game room, fitness room, and therapeutic massages. Rates in the off-season (December–April) start at $69 and go up to $119 per night; if you want a larger suite with separate sitting room, add an extra $40.

Ten minutes away is the Dutch Wonderland Amusement Park, which kids love. The park is set on 44 acres and features over 24 rides including aerial tram, high-diving shows, boat rides, bumper cars, monorail, Coney Island-type swing ride (not for the squeamish of stomachs), and roller coaster. Picnic facilities are available along the river (your kids will love watching the cows cool off in the water during the summer).

On your way back to the Strasburg Inn, stop off at Freeze 'N' Frizz for a barbecue sandwich and an Orange McFrizz (may close for winter). Don't forget to take a scenic buggy ride through the redolent Amish farmlands. And a trip to these parts is not complete until you have broken bread at Groff's Farm in Mount Joy. One word of advice here: because Groff's follows the Amish custom of presenting the seven sweets and sours on the table upon arrival, you may want to request that they withhold the chocolate cake with white icing—if you want the kids to eat a meal first.

Call 1-800-PA-DUTCH (723-8824), extension 2420, for free visitors information, discount coupons for area attractions/restaurants, and map.

Sheraton Key Largo, Florida
97000 S. Overseas Highway
Key Largo, FL 33037
(800) 826-1006 or (305) 852-5553

Only 60 miles south of Miami, this Mobil four-star award winner (six years in a row) stretches out on 12.5 beachfront acres at the start of the Florida "Key Chain." This environmentally unique property is located within a *hardwood hammock* featuring gumbo limbo and mahogany lignum vitae trees—all specially marked and lighted for nature study. The extensive Keys Kids Club program keeps kids ages 4–12 busy most of the day with banana boat rides, team scavenger hunts, nature walks, swim races, shell diving, habitat building for fish and snails, arts 'n' crafts, beach outings, movies, and snorkeling. The fee for a full day is $25; the half-day session is $15.

Additional watersports for older kids and adults include jetskiing, parasailing, Hobie-Catting, sailing, and snuba (air tanks are left on the boat so you don't have the weight of an air tank on your back). A private 21-slip marina at the hotel forms a launching pad for sport fishing, glass-bottom boat tours, private dining charters, and Champagne Sunset cruises.

The Sheraton Key Largo offers sure-saver discounts (you need to request this), which bring the rack rates down by around 40%. If you are a member of Quest, Entertainment, or ITC-50, you can get 50% off the rack rate depending upon availability. Be prepared with alternate dates to make sure you don't get locked out. AAA members can take 25% off rack rates. (Don't forget to call the discount hotel consolidators listed in this book if you're interested in reduced rates at the Sheraton Key Largo.)

Other Helpful Tidbits

Always speak up when you're traveling as a family. Particularly in the summer and around holidays, hotels often offer added freebies to entertain your kids. For example, this past summer, Radisson Hotels instituted a "Family Approved" program with participating hotels offering special children's menus, child-care services, books and games, and a delightful Radisson Crayola Kids Magic Activity Kit.

If you want more ideas on traveling with kids, consider using the services of Travel with Your Children. Managing Director Dorothy Jordon has years of experience in the family travel field. For the annual fee, you receive a quarterly newsletter, "Family Travel Times", which features first-hand anecdotes about family vacations, along with information on airlines, new resorts, etc. In addition, you can call Jordon to get information and advice about booking your trip. (Send a check for $40 to Travel with Your Children, 40 Fifth Ave. New York, NY 10011; 212-477-5524.)

CHAPTER FOUR

TOYS THAT MAKE CENTS: PLAYING THE SAVINGS GAME

Warning: These toys are recommended for adults who have difficulty swallowing large price tags.

Finding toys at true discounted prices is not much different from finding clothing, furniture, or anything else at reduced prices. Many toy companies have discount outlets or company stores where you can find excess merchandise (overruns), closeouts, package defects (toys are usually intact), change-of-packaging goods, end of promotion items, and damaged toys (not so intact) at bargain prices. Price reductions can range from as little as 20% off suggested retail to as high as 75% off retail and sometimes even more.

Stores specializing in buying up closeouts, end-of-promotion goods, and salvaged merchandise are flourishing throughout the country in the wake of store bankruptcies, closings, and the overall economic decline of retailing. Don't be a snob; always investigate these liquidators. You often can find hidden treasures at give 'em away prices (see listings later in chapter).

Even those fancy toy catalogers are affected by the economic slumps, and they don't always sell off everything in the book. What do they do with excess inventory? Find out a little later in this chapter. (Hint: you can buy up leftovers at big savings. See later listings.)

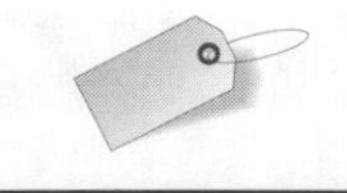

Bargain Byte

When you're bike hunting, check out Toys"Я"Us around February and the beginning of March when the store is getting ready for warmer weather and bike-buying season. The store often clears out the older, sometimes damaged, floor models to make way for new, fresher bikes. You can save from 20% to 50% off the list price by buying one of these models. We've seen defects that range from minor scratches to missing pedals. Discounts vary according to the severity of the problem. Another bonus to buying floor models is the waiving of the assembly charge, which can add another $10–$15 per bike. Not only do you save money, but you don't have to make yourself crazy figuring out how to put the darn thing together. Junior can just ride off into the sunset—happy trails.

Toys'Я'Us says that its bike coupons appear in the flyers around April or May. You can usually save around $10 with these coupons. Some toy stores even offer free helmets with bike purchases during limited-time promotions. Ask your local store whether any of these promotions are coming up.

You can even come away with some pretty good bargains at your local toy store by checking the clearance aisles, inquiring about seasonal sales, and using the in-store flyers, newspaper, or mailer coupons.

In addition, you may want to start collecting toy coupons just as you do grocery coupons. Coupons come from several sources including newspapers, in-store hand-outs, and postal mailers. Stockpile these coupons by underlining the expiration dates and filing them according to item. That way, you have the coupons ready to use for upcoming birthday presents, goody bag stuffers, holiday gifts, and emergency situations such as when a favorite toy breaks or you need a get well token. (When our daughter had an emergency appendectomy, I don't know which bill was higher—the hospital's or the toy store's.)

If you happen to come across a toy outlet that we have omitted from this guide, please let us know. We may include the outlet in a future edition.

The Games Toy Stores Play

As you recall from Chapter 1, purchasing private labels is a great way to save money on quality goods. Toy manufacturers also use private labels. One factory in China, for example, can make a particular toy that can go out under different label names and packages (some famous, some not). It's a good idea to familiarize yourself with toys in high-ticket, retail toy shops because you may find the very same toys at your local Toys'Я'Us at up to 60% less. The only difference may be the packaging, but if you're an astute shopper (and by this time you should be) you'll notice that the patent numbers are exactly the same. We recently found an adorable velcro pizza toy (under a very popular and pricey brand name) for toddlers that sold for $19.99 at one of those upscale toy boutiques. We found the exact same toy, under a different company name, at Toys'Я'Us for $7.99. The toy appeared to be identical, and the patent numbers verified our suspicions.

Where the Toy Buys Are

Believe it or not, some toy companies and toy catalogers have their own outlet stores where closeouts, defective packages, leftover goods, and damaged toys are sold at big discounts. However, if the list later in this chapter misses a company that you're interested in, do this: Look on the side of the toy box and copy down the customer service number; usually, it's a toll-free number. If you can't find the number, try calling 800 directory services. If no number is listed, talk to your local toy store manager and ask for the number; the store should have it (Toys'Я'Us is usually very good about this.) Next, call the company and speak to the customer service department. Ask if "Giggles Inc." (I made this one up) has any outlet or company stores in the U.S. Then call the store and see if you can have an item shipped to you at the outlet price. If not, keep a copy of the outlet's phone number and address in case you or a friend or relative are ever in that area.

Here's the list all you would-be Santas and Tooth Fairies have been waiting for. The list includes company store addresses, a brief description of the products available, and the range of discounts. Although some of the company stores will send out brochures, generally phone and mail orders are not accepted.

Replacing lost or broken parts is much cheaper than buying the whole toy over again. Here's a list of 800 numbers that you can call for customer assistance. In some instances, there may be a small charge for replacement parts; it's a good idea to have a major credit card ready when calling.

Brio Toys (800) 558-6863

Cap Toys (800) 562-3386

Casio (201) 361-5400

Childcraft Toys (800) 367-3255 (you also can order a toy catalog and ask about special sale items)

Constructive Playthings (U.S. Toy) (800) 255-6124

Crayola Crayons (800) CRAYOLA (Binney & Smith)

Fisher Price Toys (800) 432-5437 or (800) 527-1034

Flexible Flyer (800) 521-6233

Hasbro (800) 255-5516

Little Tikes (800) 321-0183

Mattel (800) 524-8697

Milton Bradley (413) 525-6411

Playmobil (800) PLAYMOBIL or (800) 775-8697 (Don't forget to ask about their Fun Park in Palm Beach Gardens)

Playskool (800) PLAYSKL

Toys To Grow On (sold through catalog only) (800) 542-8338

Childcraft Outlets
Midstate Mall
300 Route 18
East Brunswick, NJ 08816
(908) 613-5336

Potomac Mills
Suite 612
2700 Potomac Mills Circle
Woodbridge, VA 22192
(703) 490-3390

Tanger Factory Outlet Center
4015 35 South—Exit 200
Suite 324
San Marcos, TX 78666
(512) 392-8880

At the Childcraft outlets (part of the magic of the Walt Disney Company), you can count on an everyday minimum reduction of 30% to 75% off costumes, educational toys, apparel (Playclothes), backpacks, arts 'n' crafts kits, and more. For mail-order purposes, call the Childcraft Education Catalog at (800) 631-5652 and inquire about its sale catalogs. These catalogs feature discounts of up to 70% off regular prices on first-quality toys, clothes, and accessories.

Disney Catalog Outlets
Boaz Fashion Outlet
501 Elizabeth St.
Boaz, AL 35957
(205) 593-2400

Tanger Factory Outlet Center
2200 Tanger Blvd.
Suite 151
Gonzales, LA 70737
(504) 644-1711

Disney at a discount! You can sing "Someday my price will come." And, here it is! Right off the pages of the Disney catalogs, you can find surplus inventory at the Disney outlets offering gifts, toys, seasonal items, linens, and apparel at a minimum of 25% off catalog prices everyday (exclusive of videos and collectibles). There's nothing goofy about that! Remember to stock up on costumes for Halloween!

Economy Handicrafts
50-21 69th St.
Woodside, NY 11377-7598
(718) 426-1600

Create your own arts 'n' crafts shack and keep the kids busy on rainy days and throughout the long, hot summer with every supply imaginable from this discount warehouse. Call for a free catalog and choose from lanyards, stickers, oaktag, fabric paints, wood die-cuts, clip boards, blank visors, bulletin boards, sparkles, glitter, beads, leather purses, puzzle pins, key cases, silk screen printers, stencils, sponge art, and even a low-temperature glue gun for kids. Price breaks are given, according to the items and size of your order. You can call Economy Handicrafts and receive great tips from the staff about arts 'n' crafts birthday parties. (The craft becomes the take-home favor.) Mail and phone orders accepted.

Fisher Price Toy Store
636 Girard Ave.
East Aurora, NY 14052
(817) 354-2360

You can find the complete line of Fisher Price products here including toys, layette, clothing, and books. You also can find Mattel toys and Power Wheels, too. If you call the store's recorded message, you can learn about weekly specials that change every Monday and continue through Saturday. Some of the merchandise discounted during the week I called included Fisher Price mountain bikes and Mattel Lamborginis at 20% off, and Dance 'n' Twirl Barbies at 50% off. Discounts range from 20% to 50% off on closeouts, damaged packages, and select merchandise. However, you have to shop in person here. The store is open Mon.–Fri. 10–6; Sat. 10–5. Hours are extended around Thanksgiving and Christmas. Major credit cards and checks are accepted.

Gund Outlets
Maine Outlet
345 U.S. Route 1
Kittery, ME 03904
(207) 439-4863

Crossings Outlet Square
Tannersville, PA 18372
(717) 629-6688

Lake George Plaza
Route 9
Lake George, NY 12845
(518) 743-1970

1565 Ocean Outlets
Seaside 2
Rehoboth Beach, DE 19971
(302) 227-6631

Gotta get a Gund? Now you can get Gund stuffed animals for less at the outlet stores. You can find a dizzying selection of plush wildlife creatures at discounts of 30% to 50% off on first-quality, excess inventory, and over-stocked goods. Gund stuffed animals are among the most plush, most cuddly, and most washable of all the stuffed animals my family has snuggled with over the years. Put your name on the mailing list to receive coupons offering additional price-point reductions throughout the year. Local newspapers may also contain discount coupons, so remember to review them before you go to the outlets. Call individual stores for hours, which vary from season to season.

Hasbro Factory Store
60 Delta Drive
Pawtucket, RI 02862
(401) 431-8697

Discount toy heaven! This is a true employee store that lets the public in for these toy bargains. You can find not only Hasbro first-quality and discontinued merchandise here, but also Playskool, Kenner (where's that Easy-Bake Oven?), Parker Brothers, Milton Bradley (check out 13 Dead End Drive for the nine-year-old-and-up crowd), and Tonka, too. Everything here is discounted from 20% to 50%, so everybody wins. The store is open Mon.–Fri. 10:30–5:30. Visa and MasterCard accepted.

Hobby Surplus Sales
Mail order
(800) 233-0872

Amatos (outlet store for Hobby Surplus)
283 Main St.
New Britain, CT 06051
(203) 229-9069

All aboard for great savings on model planes, trains, and automobiles. This old-fashioned toy and hobby company stocks the largest plastic model collection in North America. For the train enthusiasts, you can find everything from limited-edition Lionel collector's sets to operating steam engines and even large-scale trains. Tracks, transformers, accessories, and repair parts are also available. If this outlet doesn't have an item, it probably doesn't exist.

Radio-controlled planes, boats, and cars, including slot cars from AC Gilbert and Tyco, are also here at great price points.

Order the catalog and save between 10% and 80% off regular retail prices throughout the year in special discount

Fact-Toy'd

Kenner's Easy-Bake Oven has been around for over 30 years, no doubt inspiring the next generation of Wolfgang Pucks, Martha Stewarts, and of course, *The Smart Shopper's* favorite, the Frugal Gourmet. More than 11 million Easy-Bake Ovens have been sold since the product's introduction in 1963.

sections. (Sale catalogs come out around four times a year.)

Visit the Amatos outlet to eye the scope of specialized inventory that you won't find at your ordinary mass merchant. Sales at the outlet store traditionally take place twice a year—in July and around Thanksgiving. The store is open Mon., Tues., Wed., Fri., and Sat. 9:30–5:30; Thurs. 9:30–7; Sun. 12–5. Visa, MasterCard, Discover, and checks are accepted.

Holt Educational Outlet
237 Riverview Ave.
Waltham, MA 02154
(617)647-0396

Phone orders accepted

Holt Everything! Here's a unique resource for toys, arts and crafts supplies, wood furniture and educational material for serious home-schoolers and interactive parents trying to raise junior's grade-point average. Browse the aisles of this warehouse-style outlet and choose from Playmobil, Brio, Crayola Educational Insights, Lego, Pacon, Gund and more at 10% to 50% off manufacturer list prices. Lots of workbooks from Frank Schaeffer, Learning Resources and other companies that will surely help your kids raise their test scores and report card grades! The store is open Thurs.–Sat. 9–5 and accepts Visa, MasterCard, checks, and cash. If you can't get to the outlet, call for a catalog.

**Kay-Bee Toy & Hobby/
Toy Works**
Pittsfield, MA (home office)
(413) 499-0086
(For a Kay-Bee or Toy Works store near you, call and ask for store operations)

The intimate Kay-Bee stores (3,000 square feet) buy closeouts and past-season toys at greatly reduced prices that are passed on to the consumer. Kay-Bee Toys has built a successful toy business specializing in value-priced closeouts and private branded goods (it also carries first-quality current goods as well). For example, last year's popular fashion doll that went for $29.99 sells for $7.99 at Kay-Bee. Other terrific deals spotted here included software closeouts from Sega and Nintendo. Kay-Bee also has an unadvertised private brand that sells for 50% less than the same comparable toys advertised through television and magazines. Especially impressive are Kay-Bee's own electronic learning aids (V-TECH) and its Teddy Precious line of teddy bears and accessories. If you're overwhelmed by the immensity and lack of service at the larger toy stores, try Kay-Bee for better prices, superior service, and a more comforting atmosphere in general. There are over 1,000 Kay-Bee stores in the U.S.

At Toy Works, a division of Kay-Bee Toys, you can find even lower prices on first-quality branded toys. Toy Works stores are located in lower-rent areas (there are approximately 70 stores in the U.S.). The average store covers about 15,000 square feet of space, much larger than a Kay-Bee store, and therefore is capable of stocking a much larger selection. As a result, these stores carry more seasonal goods such as swimming pools and bikes, plus juvenile products.

Kids Plus
70 Route 10
Whippany, NJ 07981
(201) 386-1005

When they say Kids Plus, they're not kidding. So what's the *Plus* for? You may know this discounter as a great resource for trendy kid clothes, but did you know that it also offers better-brand toys at 20%–30% off suggested retail prices? Kids Plus has now dedicated almost one-third of its selling space to great children's toys from Brio, Playmobil, Ravensburger, Lego, Duplo, K'Nex, Battat, Lamaze, Robotix, Learning Curve, Creativity, Parent's Educational Toys, and more. The store offers an extensive line of educational and infant toys usually found only in specialty toy stores. The store is open Mon.–Sat. 10–5 and accepts Visa, MasterCard, and checks.

Lilly's Kids/Lillian Vernon Outlet Stores
Loehmann's Shopping Plaza
Virginia Beach, VA 23452
(804) 463-7451

Potomac Mills
Prince William, VA 22192
(703) 491-3207

Williamsburg, VA 23788
(804) 565-1550

Old Willow Lawn Mall
Richmond, VA 23230
(804) 288-6804

Yonkers, NY 10710
(914) 961-8044

Albany, NY 12203
(518) 484-7637

Pembroke (Temporary Christmas store)
Virginia Beach, VA 23452
(804) 473-3307

Hampton, VA 23666
(804) 827-0013

Norfolk, VA 23510
(804) 622-3441

Rehoboth Beach, DE 19971
(302) 226-9227

1417 Kings Highway
Brooklyn, NY 11229
(718) 382-1761

These Lillian Vernon outlet stores claim to stock 70% of the catalog items. Call (800) 285-5555 and order the Lilly's Kids catalog to familiarize yourself with the company offerings. Then head to an outlet store where you can save between 20% and 60% off the catalog prices. Certain restrictions apply to the store products: there is no personalizing, shipping, or mailing. You can pick up some great buys including educational toys, building blocks, arts 'n' crafts paraphernalia (smocks too), dress-up trunks, dolls, diaries, closet organizers, decorative room accents, nylon totes, towels, backpacks, and on and on. Call for individual store hours and payment policies.

Mattel Toy Club
333 Continental Blvd.
El Segundo, CA 90245
(310) 252-3384

15930 East Valley Road
City of Industry, CA 91744
(818) 855-6850

15200 Trinity Blvd.
Fort Worth, TX 76155
(817) 354-2360

Operating much like the Fisher Price Store, the Mattel Toy Clubs also sell Fisher Price and Hot Wheels. Select merchandise at 20% to 50% off retail prices is listed each week on an in-store flyer. If you're willing to overlook packaging defects or crushed boxes, or buy an item without a box, you can save even more. During the week we called, Rapunzel Barbie, sans box, was selling for $9.99. Other specials included Baywatch Barbie for $6.99 and a Hot Wheels gift pack for $2.99.

Fact-Toy'd

That ubiquitous Barbie doll helps us keep track of the changing fashion and social culture. Barbie has gone through numerous careers and lifestyles running the gamut from model to veterinarian to astronaut. Since 1959, over 600 million Barbie dolls (and members of her clan) have been sold in 140 countries. Mattel sells over 20 million Barbie fashions a year, which makes it the largest producer of petite women's wear in the world!

My Precious Rose
170 Gravesend Ave.
Brooklyn, NY 11223
(718) 336-2335

Phone orders accepted

Oh, you beautiful and not-so-very-expensive doll! You may recall this entry in the fashion chapter as one of Brooklyn's premier clothing discounters, but you should also take note of its vast antique, porcelain, and collectible doll inventory at discounted prices. Hundreds of styles to choose from: Madame Alexander, Goetz, Lee Middleton, Zook, and more. Discounts on select dolls range from 20% to 50% off retail prices. The owners of this store are very knowledgeable about dolls and participate in national doll shows whenever possible. The store is open Mon.–Fri. 10–7; Sat. 10–6. All major charge cards are accepted, but no checks.

The Nature Company Outlet Stores
2700 Potomac Mills Circle
Woodbridge, VA 22193
(703) 494-8288

8155 Factory Shops Blvd.
Jeffersonville, OH 43128
(614) 948-2022

You can raise environmental consciousness without raising your family debt by shopping at this renowned retail chain's outlet. stores where you can save from 30% to 50% off on museum-type gifts for young naturalists. Choose from educational games, mask kits, puzzles, rocks, gems, jewelry kits, environmental guidebooks, and even edible crystal kits. Inventory is constantly changing depending on what overstocks and discontinued items the retail chain sends. Both stores are open Mon.–Sat. 10–9 and Sun. 11–6. Most major credit cards are accepted.

New England Hobby Supply
The Enchanted Dollhouse
(Catalog)
(800) 243-9110

The Train Exchange
(Retail store with continuous sales)
71 Hilliard St.
Manchester, CT 06040
(860) 646-0610

Dollhouses and the eensy weensy furnishings that belong inside don't come cheap. But seek and ye shall find bargains once again, courtesy of the New England Hobby Supply company, which owns The Enchanted Dollhouse and The Train Exchange. The Enchanted Dollhouse catalog features dollhouses and accessories for every age, taste, and pocketbook. To save even more money, choose from over 50 dollhouse kits and do it yourself. Oh, yes you can! The kits come with precut, furniture-grade plywood (built to last) that needs only to be glued (supplied in kit) and painted. You can choose from 96 semi-gloss colors designed specifically for dollhouses. Dollhouse kits start at $65, and these prices represent a fraction of what you would pay retail for comparable, pre-assembled dollhouses. If you can wait for the semi-annual sale catalogs, you can find additional savings ranging from 15% to 50% off dollhouse kits, select furniture, and miniatures.

If you're in the Manchester area, visit The Train Exchange located inside New England Hobby Supply's 35,000-square-foot, refurbished Victorian factory. You can find 600 different brands of indoor and outdoor model trains and accessories. Step into the "Miniature Corner" and find continuous sales of select dollhouses and furnishings throughout the year at 10% to 50% off retail prices. The Train Exchange is open Tues.–Fri. 10–8; Sat. 10–5; Sun. 1–5. You can pay for these small treasures with Visa, MasterCard, Discover, AmEx, or checks.

Odd-Job Trading
66 West 48th St.
New York, NY 10036
(212) 575-0477 (call for a store location near you)

From Baywatch Barbies to Micromachines, this store is one of the best money-saving lifesavers for parents who are sick of buying presents for those never-ending birthday parties. Odd-Job receives new shipments consisting of closeouts, end-of-promotion toys, overruns, excess inventory, and change-of-packaging goods every day. You can save at least 50% off regular retail prices and usually much more on first-quality branded name toys. If it's party favors you're after, you can find fabulous items under $2. In the past, we purchased terrific balloon-activity story books for $.29 each, girl's pastel jewelry boxes/hair and make-up organizers for $.50 cents each, Nickelodeon baseball caps for $1.29, velcro paddles and ball for under $2, and Motik building sets (like Lego) for $7.99 (regular retail goes as high as $38). Currently, there are 14 stores in the New York tri-state area.

Oriental Trading

P.O. Box 3407
Omaha, NE 68103-0407
(800) 228-2269

Free catalog
Phone and mail orders accepted

If you're new in the parenting game, get ready for years of birthday parties—which translates into a lot of goodie bags in your future. You have two ways to save on these items: you can do without them (after all, who needs friends?). Okay, so that's not an option. The next way, the best way, is to call for the free Oriental catalog and bulk order favors and gift wrap from this cornucopia of everything for parties at the lowest prices possible (we estimate around 50% less than retail, sometimes even more). If you order correctly, one box of favors can literally last for years. Our Oriental box of surprises has been in the closet for six years, and we still haven't hit bottom yet.

Here's a small list of winning favors from Oriental: stickers (one unit of 12 packages, $1.95), novelty pencils (one dozen, $1.95), sequin tiaras ($1.50 each), vinyl heart umbrellas ($3.95), plastic digital watches that really work ($1 $4 each), non-sharpening glitter pencils (one dozen, $1.80), paddle ball games (one dozen, $6), colorful mini stationery set with pencil, memo pad, sharpener, and eraser ($1.50 each), slide flutes (one dozen, $2.75), yo-yos (one dozen, $2.75), etc. The catalog also features plush animals, porcelain dolls, doll stands, puzzles, calculators, craft kits, penny candies, Power Rangers, costumes, balloons, ribbons, button covers, jewelry boxes, picture frames, gift bags, decorations, party tablecloths—in short, everything you need to make a party or bring to one, all at great savings. Seasonal/holiday catalogs are sent out on a regular basis covering Valentine's, Halloween, Easter, St. Patrick's, Christmas, etc. Oriental accepts all major credit cards.

Playmobil Fun Park & Store

8031 North Military Trail
Palm Beach Gardens, FL 33410
(407) 691-9880

Catalog available
Mail and phone orders accepted

Here's a two-part winner: while your kids are immersed in 17,000 square feet of interactive Playmobil toys, you can browse the toy store for closeout deals, saving anywhere from 30%–50% on discontinued goodies.

Your kids can try out all the Playmobil lines including victorian dollhouses, medieval castles, circuses, pirate ships, naval clippers (there's even a separate water play area for the boats), construction toys, and of course the 1,2,3 line for the wee ones still putting everything in the mouth.

In the past, Playmobil has launched several discount promotions for back-to-school, fall fever, and mid-summer, when closeouts were featured at big savings. Similar sales should continue in the future. In the meantime, look for the red neon sign leading the way to current sale items. The park and store are open Tues.–Sun. 10–6. Visa, MasterCard, AmEx, and checks are accepted. Admission to the Fun Park is free.

Stickers 'N Stuff
P.O. Box 430
Louisville, CO 80027
(303) 604-0422

Free catalog

Stick this one in your rolodex of toy bargains. If you have a kid who's stuck on sticker collecting, you will appreciate this catalog that brings down the sticker price dramatically. We loved this free catalog for the sheer variety of sticker types including sparkle prisms, pearlescents, holograms, velvet fuzzies, shiny chromes, glowing neons, scratch 'n sniffs, and hundreds more. In general, prices go for wholesale and below. Occasional closeout specials bring sticker prices down further. Stickers 'N Stuff offers *The Smart Shopper's* readers a great deal on an assortment pack of stickers. For $2.00, you get a catalog plus a set each of pearlescents, holograms, sparkling prisms, chromes, fuzzies, and thank-you teddy bears—a $7 value.

Fact-Toy'd

Here's a beary special tip: Hang on to those teddies! The Steiff Teddy Bear company was started 113 years ago by a woman who was confined to a wheelchair, and her homemade craft grew into one of the finest plush animal manufacturers in the world. A Steiff dual-plush "Petsy" bear dating circa 1920 recently went for $86,350 at the Sotheby's Grosvenor Gallery auction in London.

Toledo Physical Education Equipment
PO Box 5618
Toledo, OH 43613
(800) 225-7749

Free catalog
Phone and mail orders accepted

Parents often ask me where they can purchase professional sports and gymnastics equipment that isn't available at local sporting goods stores. Gymnasts don't progress well unless they can work out at home on a regular basis, and what better way than to install your own parallel bars, beams, horse vaults, and mats? This institutional stuff can be costly, but Toledo guarantees having the lowest prices around for the serious athlete. You can figure on an approximate 5% to 15% discount. If you find the equipment for less somewhere else, Toledo beats the price. For the ball player in your group, you can purchase the highest-quality footballs, basketballs, basketball hoops, volleyballs, soccer balls etc. Sometimes you get free shipping for volleyballs and footballs. Call for the free catalog. You can pay by Visa or MasterCard.

Totally Toys
Foxmoor Village Outlet
Box 6E
East Stroudsburg, PA 18301
(717) 223-1616

Phone orders accepted

Those hard-to-find discounted Playmobil and Brio toys are here at 20%–25% off retail, and Totally Toys will be totally happy to ship them directly to you. This specialty toy store carries a full line of educational toys, personalized novelty items from barrettes to pencils, and a collection of limited edition porcelain dolls (including porcelain Barbies and a full line of Betty Boop). Hard-to-get, high-quality Amish wooden toys from doll cradles to high chairs are designed exclusively for Totally Toys and will probably last through several generations. You also can pick up Lego here at discounted prices. Hours vary depending on the time of year, but the store is generally open seven days a week. Totally Toys will totally accept your Visa, MasterCard, and AmEx for payment.

Tower Hobbies
Catalog and Super Saver Club
P.O. Box 778
Champaign, IL 61820
(800) 637-4989

Call for the annual 300-page catalog and you'll understand why Tower Hobbies is considered the largest radio-controlled vehicle house in the world. You can find replicas of the hottest big boy toys including cars, boats, planes, jeeps, helicopters, slot cars, and all the support equipment that goes with them. Every two months you receive 50- to 70-page sale catalogs featuring greatly reduced prices. If you join the Super Saver Club (annual membership fees range from $19.99 to 29.99), you receive additional discount coupon booklets, technical updates, newsletters, and product reviews. You also gain access to greatly reduced scratch 'n' dent items as well as discontinueds. Tower guarantees that if you don't save the cost of the membership fee in your purchases, it will credit the fee back to you.

The Toy Store
Putnam Park
254 Canal St.
Brattleboro, VT 03501
(802) 257-5846

Phone orders accepted

Choose from a menagerie of cuddly stuffed critters from Mary Meyer's at this factory store where parents rush for plush at 15% to 70% off retail prices. Love those walking, talking, and smart mouth M&Ms? They're here in an assortment of colors and sizes; there's even one so large that an average adult may have difficulty dragging it out of the store. Lots of bears are here including the famous Green Mountain Collection. We also noticed Tucker Turtle, which tucks in and out of the shell and was the Parent's Choice Honor winner of 1991. If you can't get to the store but you know what you want, the factory can ship items. The store is open seven days a week; store hours vary according to the season. Visa, MasterCard, Discover, and checks are accepted.

Toy Liquidators/
Amazing Toys/
Toys Unlimited
(800) 218-7160

The Loehmanns of the toy industry, this off-price toy chain discounts branded toys from 30% to 70% off retail. You can find closeouts, discontinueds, and leftover fun stuff from Mattel, Tyco, Fisher Price, Little Tikes, Kenner, Playskool, and many other manufacturers. You can find these toy havens in outlet malls and strip centers throughout the U.S. Call the 800 number for a store near you. Visa, MasterCard, Discover accepted, but no Monopoly money.

CHAPTER FIVE

FAMILY DINING WITHOUT RESERVATIONS: FIVE-STAR CHEFS SHOW YOU HOW

Who doesn't love to eat out at wonderful restaurants where you can experience the latest culinary creations from America's top chefs? Unfortunately, many people stop enjoying these gourmet adventures once they have children. Instead of contemplating trying a tempting dessert, parents wonder what their kids will eat, whether they'll behave and what the bill will be. This chapter will show you how to eat out with the kids without reservations—your reservations, that is.

If you're still not convinced that kids and fine dining go together, the second part of this chapter will show you how to prepare gourmet goodies at home. You'll save money by eating at home, and you'll also help your children develop a more sophisticated palate while expanding their food horizons. Then, when you do go out to eat as a family, everyone will have a more palatable time.

We approached some of America's hottest cookbook authors, restaurateurs, hotel chefs and food personalities and asked them to contribute special gourmet kid recipes along with dining tips to *The Smart Shopper's Guide*. To all these stars in the culinary arts who participated, we thank you from the bottom of our stomachs.(And for those who would like to be included in future editions, we'd love to hear from you!)

Here's the dilemma: There are going to be times when you'll find yourself eating at more upscale restaurants with the kids. Just because you can't get a babysitter doesn't mean you have to settle for maintenance feeding (hamburgers, hot dogs, chicken nuggets, pizza etc.) every time you have a meal out with the brood. When you're on vacation, you're missing out if you don't sample some of the trendy eateries or local bistros! Dining out with the family in tow doesn't have to drain your bank account or your nerves. Here's some food for thought:

- **To the manners born.** No matter how young your baby, it's never too early to enroll him or her in Restaurant 101. If you enjoy eating out, then it's imperative to take newborns, infants and kids out on a regular basis to learn proper restaurant etiquette. If you're worried about the unavoidable toddler messes, you may want to bring your own plastic dropcloth to drape underneath the seat. For older kids, it's a good idea to bring a backpack of travel-sized games, activity books, small crafts kits, a walkman with tapes or CDs and perhaps some teen magazines to keep them occupied while waiting for the meal.

Food Byte

Tiny bubbles can fill up tiny stomachs faster than you can say "check please!" If you want your child to sit at the table eating a complete meal with the rest of the family, tell the waiter to hold off bringing the sodas until the meal is served, or perhaps halfway into the dinner. I guarantee you, if you let your child drink soda before the meal arrives, he or she will eat very little food. Consequently, your kid is likely to get bored and that's the end of your pleasant dinner.

- **Don't order down the menu—from soup to dessert—for a child.** Kids don't need a five-course meal. In fact, you can save a substantial amount of money by foregoing the entree altogether. Considering everything that will eventually be on the table—crudités, salads, rolls and, of course, your food—you should order only an appetizer for your child. In some restaurants, appetizers are so large that they can easily be shared by two children. Ask the waiter how large the portion is, and ask that it be divided in the kitchen to avoid any problems at the table.

- **If the appetizers aren't so appetizing and there's nary a kids' menu in sight, don't fret!** Ask the waiter to bring you a 'monkey dish' (small saucer-like plate) serving of one of the entrees or side dishes. If this terminology doesn't work, simply ask for a child-size portion at a lower price. Generally, you'll be charged 35% to 50% off the menu price. Keep in mind that restaurants want you to return and will do whatever it takes to make you happy, so speak up!

- **BYOM—Bring your own kid's meal.** When in doubt, wrap up favorite foods from home, or even stop in at a local pizza place and take a couple of slices to the restaurant. A hungry kid is a cranky kid, and there may be times when you might not be able to find anything on the menu for a picky eater who's resistant to unfamiliar food.
- **The early bird family catches the savings.** Early bird specials are not just for senior citizens and retired people. They're ideal for families who need to eat early and save money in the process. These complete dinners, at lower prices, are generally large enough to share easily with children. If you need to, just order an extra side dish or appetizer to fill in. Let the kids have the dessert that comes with the meal; you don't need it anyway.
- **Join a dining club.** Patronize restaurants listed in their directories for savings of 10% to 50% off meals. (Some examples are Dine A Mate, Transmedia, Entertainment, IGT etc. See Chapter 3 for a complete listing.) Make sure to have your membership card with you at all times. It's also a good idea to keep a copy of the directory in the glove compartment of your car for easy access and last-minute dining decisions.

Bargain Byte

Transmedia offers two discount dining programs. One program charges an annual fee of $50, which allows you to deduct 25% off the total food bill (exclusive of alcohol, tax and tips) at participating establishments. The other program offers a free (yes, *free*) lifetime membership to Transmedia provided that you use the card and charge a minimum of $200 per year in dining expenses. The discount here is 20% off your total food bill—a bit lower, but still a pretty good deal. Call (800) 422-5090 for information and applications.

- **Need to kill a little time while waiting for the food to arrive?** In our family, we play a little game called, "Let's Inspect the Bathroom." Actually, this one was inspired by my sister Lori (you know, the one who had the grisly bed-jumping accident from the furniture chapter, and the one who taught me how to find out about lower hotel rack rates in the travel section). When Lori was a little girl, she had a thing about strange bathrooms, an unyielding curiosity that obligated someone to take her into the lavatory for a quick look-see. It kept her quiet, it wasted time—in short, it worked. Remembering this, I decided to turn my daughter on to the wonders of strange bathrooms. Keep in mind, upscale restaurants usually go hand-in-hand with upscale bathrooms. Point out exotic fixtures, floral arrangements, potpourri aromas, marble designs (here's a good opportunity to give a painless lesson on geometric tesselations—look it up), and of course, self-flushing and automatic seat-covering toilets are truly magical. You can improvise with each individual bathroom's special features.

Let's Get Cooking with Celebrity Chefs . . . It's Cheaper than Eating Out

Let's face it, maintenance feeding and cooking is a big bore. The goal here is to teach your children about all the wonderful flavors and food combinations beyond hamburgers and chicken nuggets. The sooner you begin this process, the sooner the kids will appreciate fine dining and look forward to eating out at glamorous, grown-up restaurants. The following recipes are provided by some of the country's most renowned and gifted chefs to help you get started on this exciting family food adventure.

The recipe listings begin with desserts. As my favorite bumper sticker reads, "Life is uncertain, eat dessert first." What kid wouldn't agree?

The Mansion on Turtle Creek

Recipe by Dean Fearing

This candy bar cake is addictive. Believe me! Created by renowned chef Dean Fearing of the Mobil five-star and Triple AAA five-diamond resort The Mansion on Turtle Creek in Dallas, this culinary treat can be easily whipped up at home. Don't forget to tell the kids that great desserts like this one can't be found at fast food joints, but rather at nicer restaurants where they may have to mind their manners a bit more. Once the kids have tasted incredible treats like this one, they'll be begging you to take them out to eat.

Heath Bar Cake

Dedicated to anyone who loves Heath Bars:

1 cup packed light brown sugar
1/2 cup sugar
1/2 cup unsalted butter, softened
1 large egg, beaten
1 cup buttermilk
1 teaspoon pure vanilla extract
2 cups sifted all-purpose flour
1 teaspoon baking soda
8 Heath Bars, frozen and chopped
1/2 cup chopped pecans

Preheat oven to 350 degrees. Grease and flour a 13 × 9 × 2 inch cake pan. In a mixing bowl, cream sugars and butter. When well mixed, beat in egg and slowly add buttermilk. Beat in vanilla, flour and baking soda. Pour into prepared pan. Sprinkle candy and nuts over top. Bake in preheated oven for 45 minutes or until a cake tester inserted in the center comes out clean. Cool on wire rack. Slice before heating using a serrated knife. Wrap in foil and warm at 350 degrees for 10 to 15 minutes. Serve immediately. Keep remaining cake tightly covered to retain moisture for future servings. At The Mansion, the Heath Bar Cake is served with chocolate and caramel topping, along with a dollop of whipped cream or vanilla ice cream.

Yield: One 13 × 9 × 2-inch cake

Loews Santa Monica

Recipe by Francisco Lozano, Pastry Chef

Every night at bedtime, the lucky children who stay at the Loews Santa Monica Hotel in California are treated to the most scrumptious chocolate chip cookies on the planet. The cookies are accompanied by a glass of cold milk served in a ceramic cow. I was so excited about these cookies that I literally begged the kitchen for the recipe, which I'm now pleased to share with you. This must be what Sesame Street's Cookie Monster had in mind all the time.

"C" is for cookie, Loews Santa Monica Chocolate Chip Cookie that is!

The Loews Santa Monica Chocolate Chip Cookies

1 cup of shortening
1 cup of butter (softened to room temperature)
2 cups brown sugar
1 cup granulated sugar
4 eggs
5 cups all-purpose flour
1 teaspoon baking soda
2 cups chocolate and/or white chocolate chips (author's note: I prefer to combine them, 1 cup each)
2 cups walnuts
1/2 cup melted chocolate
2 teaspoons vanilla extract
1 teaspoon salt

In an electric mixer, beat butter and shortening until creamy, add both sugars and beat at medium speed. Add eggs and mix until combined; add flour, baking soda and salt. Then, add chocolate chips, nuts, melted chocolate and vanilla extract. Mix at low speed until combined. Scoop the cookie dough and chill for about an hour. Bake at 350 degrees for about 10–12 minutes or until golden brown.

Yield: 2 dozen cookies

Aureole, The Lenox Room, and Alva (New York City)

Recipe by Charlie Palmer, Chef/Owner

Aureole is legendary as one of New York City's shining star dining establishments. Zagat's restaurant guide lists Aureole as #1 in New York City for American cuisine. If you're passionate about desserts, Aureole's architecturally inspired sweets are as exquisite to look at as they are to eat.

The chef and owner of Aureole, The Lenox Room, and Alva—Charlie Palmer—is also a father of two little boys. Palmer, who believes in exposing children to the finer things in life (including exotic foods), has devised some strategies to make fine dining in the world's most notable eateries a painless and even pleasant experience. Charlie's first suggestion is that you go as early as possible, preferably when the doors open, before the dining crowd arrives. This way you don't have to worry about annoying other customers. You might even want to call ahead just to make sure that kids are welcome at the restaurant. Palmer also suggests that you order immediately and share with the children. There's no better way to expand little tastebuds than to allow kids to sample unusual fare.

Charlie Palmer's Orange Sorbet Oranges

6 large, juicy oranges (such as Valencias)
1 lemon
1 cup sugar
1/2 cup of wildflower honey
1 1/2 cups water
1 egg white

Wash, dry and roll the oranges on a table to loosen them a bit. Cut the oranges in half horizontally. Using a spoon, scoop out the flesh of the orange, taking care to keep the skin in one piece. Line up the empty shells on a tray.

Squeeze and reserve all the juice from the orange flesh into a large measuring cup—you should have between 2 1/4 – 2 3/4 cups of juice (add more if you need to).

Combine the juice of the lemon with the sugar, honey and water in a sauce pot and simmer over medium heat for about 20 minutes—you should have approximately 1 1/2 cups of liquid. Cool and combine with the orange juice and 1 whipped egg white.

Place mixture in an ice cream freezer and freeze to the specs of the machine.

When the sorbet is ready, remove it and fill the orange shells level to the top. Cover with film and place in a freezer.

When you are ready to serve, take a hot, serrated knife and cut each orange shell into three wedges, returning them to the freezer until they are all cut. Serve 3–4 wedges on a small plate and garnish with a sprig of mint.

The Peaks At Telluride

This forward-thinking, world-class resort in Telluride, Colorado has created an innovative KidSpa program where kids learn relaxation techniques along with the wonders of spa cuisine. Here's an appealing recipe from The Peaks At Telluride that you'll want to tell your kids about. In fact, kids will have a great time helping to cut out the circles, stuff in the bananas, dunk the bread in the egg mixture and more when you make this delicious departure from the usual French Toast breakfast recipe.

Banana French Toast

4 slices cinnamon raisin bread, 1 inch thick
2 medium (6 oz.) bananas, peeled
4 eggs
1/4 cup milk
1 tablespoon sugar
1 1/2 teaspoons cinnamon
pinch nutmeg
4 tablespoons unsalted butter
8 strawberries, rinsed and sliced as needed
maple syrup

Pre-heat an electric griddle to medium (if you have one) or use a large skillet if you don't. With a round 1 1/4-inch cutter, cut two holes in each slice of bread and lay the slices out on a counter. Cut the bananas into fourths and place a piece in each hole (each section of banana will be approximately 1 1/4 inches long). Using the palm of your hand, press the bananas down until they are flush with the bread (the bananas will be firmly lodged in the holes). In a shallow dish, beat together eggs, milk, sugar, vanilla, cinnamon and nutmeg. Soak each slice of bread in the egg mixture for 4–5 minutes, turning the slices at least once so they will be evenly moistened.

Heat the butter on the griddle, or in the skillet, and when it sizzles, remove the slices from the egg mixture and place on the heat. Cook each side approximately 3–4 minutes, or until golden brown. Place immediately on warm plates, sprinkle with the sliced strawberries, and serve with warm maple syrup.

Lo Mein with Sesame and Peanuts

Recipe by Martha Kimmel, author of "Mommy Made And Daddy Too! Home Cooking for a Healthy Baby & Toddler" (Bantam, $14.95)

"A friend in my neighborhood stopped me the other day and asked what she could do about her three-year-old son who had insisted on eating peanut butter and jelly for lunch every day for the past two months. I explained that temporary food fixations are very popular in the younger set and would not make him sick. To help break this kind of spell, try getting your little one involved in the food-making process. Have him help you plan the menus and shop for the food. When it comes time to prepare the meal, have him help you here, too. Certainly he could assist in making tuna fish salad, form a hamburger patty, clean lettuce, snap beans, or even help in scrambling eggs. Not only will this help instill a new interest in other foods, but it will give your little one a new sense of independence.

If peanut butter is a favorite in your home like it is in ours, the following recipe will give new credibility to the old standby."

—Martha Kimmel.

Any bright vegetables on hand: a little grated carrot, strips of red bell pepper, snow peas etc., will add additional color and crunch to these oriental-inspired noodles. Prepared with whole wheat pasta, this recipe provides complete protein. Any pasta shape can be used, but linguine or spaghetti is traditional.

Lo Mein with Sesame and Peanuts

3 tablespoons peanut oil
1/4 teaspoon light sesame oil
2 tablespoons peanut butter (crunchy or smooth)
2 tablespoons soy sauce
1 tablespoon water
1 medium garlic clove, crushed
1/2 pound whole wheat or regular linguine or spaghetti, cooked according to package directions
3 scallions, trimmed and thinly sliced
1/2 cucumber, peeled, seeded, thinly sliced

Combine peanut and sesame oils in a large bowl. Add peanut butter, soy sauce, water and garlic and mix well with a whisk to blend. Drain pasta well and toss with dressing. Garnish with scallion and cucumber.

Yield: 5 cups

Dive! (Steven Spielberg and Jeffrey Katzenberg, part-owners)

Recipes by Michael O' Donovan, Executive Chef for Dive!

Could there be a kid-friendlier restaurant than one inspired and created by Steven Spielberg? I don't think so. From the moment you set eyes on the phantasmagorical sight of a life-size submarine crashed into a wall of the restaurant, you know you're in for more than a meal. When my family visited this cornucopia of Spielbergian special effects (such as fiberoptic accents, continuous video "dive" shows on a seamless, 16 cube video wall, clanging bells, exposed conduits that actually burst with steam, working periscopes, vibrating banquettes etc.), we were delighted with the excellent quality of the food. It seems that Mr. Spielberg was having trouble finding his favorite, hometown submarine sandwiches in the Los Angeles area, despite some comprehensive research. So he decided to create a restaurant that specialized in submarines, but not just any ordinary sub; his are gourmet versions!

Michael O'Donovan, executive chef for all Dive! restaurants (Los Angeles, Las Vegas, Barcelona) suggests that if you're eating out at a restaurant that doesn't cater to kids, or if you're unfamiliar with the menu, you should call ahead and ask the chef's advice. Donovan says that any "good" restaurant will help with a child's meal. He also advocates teachers to arrange field trips of restaurant kitchens with a chef on hand to show the kids how meals are prepared.

So let's Dive! right in to some of Dive!'s innovative kid treats!

Carrot Chips

(wouldn't Roger Rabbit love these?)

4 large carrots
6 cups of canola oil
$^1/_2$ teaspoon granulated sugar
1 pinch of cinnamon

Peel the carrots and slice them as thin as possible. The preferred method is to use a food processor. Set the carrot chips aside, then heat the canola oil to a temperature of 275 degrees. Carefully place the carrot chips into the hot oil for approximately 4 minutes, turning continuously. When the carrot chips are cooked, turn them out onto a napkin or paper towel and allow them to drain, then sprinkle with the sugar and cinnamon, or eat them plain. The carrot chips may also be submerged in your favorite dip such as French onion. They are a great substitute for potato chips.

Veggie Hero Sandwich

(Could this be the veggie sandwich that inspired Spielberg's hero Indiana Jones?)

1 oz black olive spread
1 oz goat cheese
2 ozs roasted red pepper
1 oz thinly sliced red onion marinated in balsamic vinegar
1 oz cleaned spinach leaf
4 slices of Roma tomatoes

In a 6-inch piece of crusty French bread, spread the goat cheese and olive spread on opposite sides of the bread. Then simply arrange the rest of the ingredients on the bread. You can substitute any vegetable for another.

S'Mores

(You know E.T. would have phoned home for these!)

2 graham crackers
1 chocolate bar
8 marshmallows
$^1/_2$ oz chocolate syrup

Place the chocolate bar on top of the graham crackers and melt in the microwave oven for 8 seconds. Place marshmallows on melted chocolate and close like a sandwich. Drizzle chocolate sauce and refrigerate.

Cheeca Lodge's Atlantic Edge Restaurant Islamorada, Florida

Recipes by Dawn Sieber, Executive Chef

One of the most fabulous dining spots in the Florida Keys is at Cheeca Lodge's Atlantic Edge restaurant. This eatery is so popular that it's not unusual to see helicopters landing on the hotel's golf course, bringing in hungry clients from southern parts of the U.S. Executive chef of the Atlantic Edge, Dawn Sieber, herself a mother, offers Smart Shoppers this recipe for what kids may think of as a large gourmet fish stick, but in reality is the much more sophisticated and very delicious: "Presidential Snapper."

The Presidential Snapper

(Yellowtail snapper encrusted in Yucca with Roasted Pepper-Orange Salsa and Sizzling Black Beans)

2 pounds (about 4 medium) yucca (potatoes such as Cheff's or Malagas may be substituted just remember to grate and use immediately)
4 each 7-8 oz yellowtail (or other type) snapper filets (skin on)
4 each Florida oranges (peeled and sectioned, no pits)
2 each Key limes (juiced)
1/2 bunch cilantro
10 ozs extra-virgin olive oil salt and pepper to taste
1 each eggplant (sliced in eight rounds and grilled or sauteéd in olive oil)
1 cup cooked black beans

Peel yucca and grate fine. Season fish and grated yucca with salt and pepper. Press and mold grated yucca on to snapper, opposite the skin side. Heat sauteé pan and place snapper carefully yucca side down in 4 ounces of olive oil. Cook until golden brown and then turn and finish cooking skin-side down. Place on sliced grilled eggplant.

For Salsa:

Mix orange sections, diced roasted pepper, lime juice, four ounces extra-virgin olive oil, chopped cilantro, salt and pepper to taste. Place salsa on top of yucca snapper.

For Sizzling Black Beans:

Wash and dry black beans. Heat 2 ounces olive oil very hot and toss dry cooked beans. Just prior to serving, garnish salsa-topped fish with sizzling black beans and cilantro sprig.

Key Lime Pie from Cheeca Lodge

(Where better to get a recipe for Key Lime Pie than from the Keys where it originated?)

4 eggs
1 cup sugar
3/4 cup lime juice
1/2 cup butter
1 teaspoon gelatin, softened in cold water
zest of two limes

Combine all ingredients except gelatin, whisk together and cook over hot water until thick. Remove from heat, stir in gelatin. Pour into graham cracker crust. Chill. Top with whipped cream.

Graham Cracker Crust

1 1/2 cups graham cracker crumbs
1/2 cup sugar
6 tablespoons melted butter

Press into pan.

The Horseradish Grill—Atlanta, Georgia

Voted one of the best restaurants of 1995 by *Bon Apetit* magazine and critically acclaimed as one of the most outstanding, authentic Southern cuisine establishments in the U.S., you might have to wait up to two hours to eat here. But, now, you can sample some of the Grill's recipes at home!

Pan-fried chicken, one of the Grill's specialties, takes some time to prepare. As great things never come easy, just consider this the Tiffany diamond of southern fried chicken. Just do it! Your kids will thank you.

Horseradish Grill Fried Chicken

3 pounds cut-up, bone-in chicken or single parts like thighs
2 quarts cold water
1/2 cup kosher salt
1 quart buttermilk
1 1/2 cups all-purpose flour
1 1/2 teaspoon fine sea salt
1/2 teaspoon freshly ground pepper
1/4 cup cornstarch
2 tablespoons potato flour
1 pound lard
1/4 pound unsalted butter
1/4 pound smoked bacon

Rinse the chicken pieces under cool running water. In a large bowl, mix the water and kosher salt, stirring until the salt is dissolved. Immerse the chicken in the salted water and refrigerate for 4 hours or overnight.

Pour the buttermilk into a large bowl. Remove the chicken pieces from the salt water soak and transfer them to the buttermilk bath. Let them soak refrigerated for 4 hours or overnight.

Remove the chicken pieces from the buttermilk, holding each piece above the bowl, so excess buttermilk drains off. Lay each piece on a wire cooling rack.

In a large bowl, mix the flour, sea salt, pepper, cornstarch and potato flour. One by one, dredge the chicken pieces in the flour, shaking off excess. Lay each coated piece on the cooling rack.

In a large cast-iron or other heavy skillet, melt the lard and butter. Add the bacon. When the lard and butter mix is very hot, but not smoking, use tongs to add the chicken pieces in a single layer. It may be necessary to cook the chicken in two batches. The pieces should be half submerged in the cooking fat. Regulate the fat so it just bubbles, and cook each piece for 10 to 12 minutes per side, turning once, or several times if needed, to brown evenly. The total cooking time should be about 25 minutes. With a sharp paring knife, cut to the bone of one piece to make sure it cooked through.

Remove the cooked chicken to the cooling rack or drain it on crumbled up paper towels. Serve warm or at room temperature.

The Horseradish Grill welcomes children. When the little ones are expected, the staff simply throws some paper tablecloths over the linens, adds a few crayons, and you've got the beginning of a memorable feast. For dessert, these clever restaurateurs bring out warm cupcakes and let the kids do the frosting and finishing!

Here's the recipe for The Horseradish Grill's number one dessert for kids.

Chocolate Chocolate Cake

Cake:

2 cups granulated sugar
1 1/2 cups all-purpose flour
1/2 teaspoon salt
3/4 teaspoon baking soda
4 ounces unsweetened chocolate, chopped
1 cup hot double-strength brewed coffee (may substitute with decaf coffee)
1/2 cup vegetable oil
2 eggs, room temperature
1 1/2 teaspoons pure vanilla extract
1/2 cup sour cream, at room temperature

Frosting:

1 cup heavy cream
1 stick unsalted butter
1/3 cup granulated sugar
1/4 teaspoon salt
1 pound semisweet chocolate, chopped
1 teaspoon pure vanilla extract
1/4 cup double-strength brewed coffee (may substitute decaf coffee)

Preheat oven to 325 degrees. Butter and flour two 9-inch cake pans. In a bowl, sift together sugar, flour, salt and baking soda, set aside. Stir 4 ounces chocolate into the hot coffee and allow to melt completely. In a large bowl, mix together the oil, eggs, vanilla and sour cream. Stir in the melted chocolate mixture and blend well. Add the flour mixture in 1/3 increments, stirring well after each addition.

Divide batter among prepared cake pans, and bake for 30–40 minutes, or until a cake tester inserted in the center comes out clean.

Frosting:

Heat the cream, butter, sugar and salt over low heat until butter is melted. Remove from heat and stir in chocolate until melted and smooth. Add vanilla and coffee, stir until blended. Allow mixture to cool to room temperature and to a spreadable consistency. Frost the top of one layer, top with second layer, then frost the top and sides.

Yield: 10 servings

If you're planning a visit to The Horseradish Grill with kids, call ahead and find out what the best day and time would be to bring them so you can bypass any extended wait, which could prove to be disastrous with kids. Once there, you must try at least one of their unique, homemade ice creams from peanut brittle to apple cider! If you don't, someone will be coming to your home to confiscate this book.

Los Abrigados Resort & Spa— Sedona, Arizona

Here's another contemporary, world-class resort that knows how to please kids both in and out of the restaurants. Apart from a novel children's menu, this hotel knows the importance of eye-catching presentation and cleverly serves many kid meals on a genuine frisbee that kids can later take home with them. Another innovative, keep 'em quiet and happy at the dinner table trick is the "Lazer Gazers." Once the kids finish eating and mom and dad want to linger over their meal a bit longer, the children remain seated, don the glasses, gazing at all the lights, color prisms and reflections, while parents finish up and wait for the check! Executive chef at Los Abrigados, Scott Uehlein, suggests that children be offered samples of adult meal selections to broaden their culinary horizons. Uehlein has come up with the following, a simple, interactive and easily consumed breakfast item that he developed with the help of his two-year old daughter. Uehlein describes this as, "The perfect dish! My two-year-old loves to help make her own breakfast in the morning using this easy recipe and the microwave."

Easy Cheesy Egg

1 Egg
2 tablespoons shredded cheese
salt and pepper

In a bowl, mix the egg, cheddar cheese, salt and pepper. Spray a microwave-safe cup (a tea cup works great) with a little cooking spray, and pour in egg mixture. Microwave 1 minute on medium-high power. Carefully remove, and turn egg over. Microwave for 40 additional seconds. Kids love watching the egg cook.

CHAPTER SIX

BORN TO BE STYLED

Newborns are such a pleasure to dress. They never argue and seem to be happy in any ridiculous little thing you put them in. Rompers, bubbles, and jumpsuits flatter any baby. But not every color complements every baby. For my child, the color choices were limited to baby pink, lavender, or white (I never liked babies in that 1950's shade of mint green). I must add that unless you're in some way related to the Addams Family, keep your sweet infants out of basic black! They basically look terrible in it. The little cuties just don't have strong enough color to make it work, and they're too young to wear make-up. Stick to baby pastels and primary colors.

The trouble seems to begin when those darling little creatures become mobile. I'll never understand why some parents insist on dressing their crawling daughters in lacy dresses that are sure to get caught under the knees and trip them up (granted they don't have far to fall).

As your child grows older, you need to use some critical thinking skills and assess your child's physical assets and deficits in order to help them look their best. It's up to you, the parent, to help your kids get a sense of their own individual style. How important is it that your child look good? Should we place so much emphasis on outward beauty? Does this preoccupation with physical looks qualify us as nominees for the Hall of Fame for the Terminally Shallow? Consider this study from the March 1992 issue of *Children's Business* based on a Utah State University survey: "What a kid wears can influence an adult's impression of that child's ability to do such things as jump rope and solve math problems. Fashionable clothing lent an air of competence, especially to attractive boys and unattractive girls. By paying attention to what kids wear, parents can modify the important first impression kids project on teachers." You know the expression, "you are what you eat?" Well, you and the kids are what you wear, at least to the rest of the shallow world at large that judges kids (and you, too) based on how they look.

When I appear on television and radio programs, I am inevitably asked, "If there's one vital piece of styling advice you can give to parents, what would that be?" My response is always, "Don't be fooled by 'hanger appeal.'" Some outfits look terrific on the hanger, but you need to ask yourself if this silhouette would flatter your child. If so, have your child try the garment on. Now, step away from your child and look at him or her. I mean *really* look. Ask yourself, "Does this outfit do anything for my child, or does it just hang on her?" Perhaps all it needs is a petticoat; ask the salesperson for one and see if it makes a difference. (If you're shopping specifically for dresses, it's a good idea to bring a petticoat from home, in case the store doesn't have one.) One pet peeve of mine is little girls in oversized dresses that are way too long and shapeless. Whenever I see a girl dressed in one of these, I want to shake her mother and ask, "What were you thinking?" Kids have such natural beauty that it's a shame to detract from that.

The same principle applies to boys. Try on outfits, step back, and evaluate. Boys do not look great in everything and every color. Little boys with very thin legs should not wear those baggy, oversized, grandpa shorts, and they certainly shouldn't accessorize this mess with heavy, clunky athletic shoes. Whenever I see this look, I want to cry. A shorter, more tapered Bermuda short and a lighter deck sneaker would be much more becoming and also help the kid look a little heavier. Nothing makes a thin kid look thinner than oversized clothes and Herman Munster footwear.

Here's Looking at You, Kid!

I have used years of experience styling kids of all shapes, sizes, hair lengths, and temperaments for print and television to compile the following list of *Smart Shopper's* styling do's and don'ts. After all, a bargain isn't a bargain if your kid doesn't look great in it.

Don'ts

- Don't overwhelm your child with the latest trends, glitz, and oversized hair ornaments (they always remind me of the Flying Nun, and I am forever awaiting take-off). A simple and somewhat classic look allows a child's natural beauty to shine through.
- If your child has legs like Olive Oyl, combat boot looks are not for them. Stick to lighter, more delicate footwear. For girls, you might want to try T-straps, ghilly ties, Mary Janes, multi-strap flats, or slip-on ballet styles. For boys, deck shoes, loafers, and Converse-like basketball hi-tops work well. (The hi-top tends to flatter a thin leg by accentuating calf musculature by cutting the leg at a point that contributes to the illusion of a heavier leg.)
- For a fuller-figured child, stick to drop-waist dresses and tops that tend to elongate the torso giving a thinner appearance. Do stay away from fuller skirts that accentuate the hips, making the child appear larger than she actually is. (Obviously, these items would be a good choice for the thinner child.)
- Unless you've trained with Jose Eber or Vidal Sassoon, do not attempt to cut and style your child's hair; they won't sit still and you don't have a clue anyway. Here's where it doesn't pay to skimp on the pennies. Let a professional cut your child's hair. Remember, a great outfit doesn't look so great with a ratty looking head of hair on top of it. And no, you probably

can't cut a straight bang. While we're on the subject of bangs, make sure the bangs are not cut too far back into the crown. What you end up with are two haircuts in one: a short haircut and a long one. This always looks ridiculous. Make sure the stylist doesn't go too far beyond your child's natural hairline. Also, if your child ever decides to grow her bangs out, it won't be such a major ordeal. You won't have half a head of hair to grow out, but rather a small portion of hair that can easily be managed with headbands or clips.

- Keep clogs and Birkenstocks away from children. These shoes belong on adults who eat macrobiotic foods (not that there's anything wrong with that) and fondly recall Woodstock (wait a minute, that would be me). Small children with little feet always look so overwhelmed by bulky sandals, and open-back clogs on active kids are an accident waiting to happen. I saw a little girl running down the stairs in a pair of clogs that got away from her. She tumbled down the stairs and was badly hurt. If you still insist on this look for your kids, you're better off purchasing those clogs and Birkies with a sling back that may help to prevent chipped teeth, skinned knees, fractured wrists, sprained ankles, and other mishaps that can occur when running kids fall out of open-backed clogs.
- Kids and paisleys don't mix.
- Less is more—especially where kids fashion is concerned. Simple elegance will always be in. Let the fabric and style shine through. Stay away from poly/cotton ensembles with enough embellishments and ornamentation to set off the metal detector at the airport.
- Don't let your kid live in white sneakers. They simply don't look great with everything. Nurses and orderlies have no choice—your child should.
- Keep bow ties away from little boys. Bow ties belong on little boys with wooden bodies and pull strings at the back of their

heads. The only live boys who should be permitted to wear bow ties are those whose birth certificates indicate Steve Urkel as the child's legal name.

- It may not be stylish, but if your child is not potty-trained, put a diaper on under his or her bathing suit. Do not treat the pool as a community toilet.
- Don't experiment with new hair cuts and hair styles right before a special event or picture-taking day. This is a surefire formula for disaster. Stick to what you know and feel comfortable with. If your child has never worn curls, don't take that curling iron out now or your daughter could end up looking like a poodle, or worse, you could burn her fragile hair. Take the time to read instructions carefully when you use electronic curling and straightening tools. In fact, I always remove curlers and irons a little early, just to make sure I'm not damaging the hair shaft. Also, if you smell something burning or feel that something is wrong, remove styling tools from your child's hair immediately.

Do's

- All kids look great in navy.
- Hi-top Converse-like sneakers look terrific on all kids and coordinate well with many different looks. Buy an assortment of colors. (They're available at Syms, Marshalls, and TJ Maxx at bargain prices from $8 to $12, compared to regular retail prices ranging from $28 to $36.) Hi-tops add a funky twist to retro and vintage dressing if accessorized right.
- Iron, mom or dad! Kids look 1000% better when an outfit is well-pressed. The clothing will hang properly, and your child looks neat and fashionable.
- Always bring your child along for fittings. You can't buy shoes, headbands, or hats for your kids unless they try them on. No

two heads—or feet—are shaped alike. Therefore, the fit and look will be different on all kids.

Size Wise

You probably have a range of clothing sizes in your closet—even if you haven't gained or lost weight. Different manufacturers' sizes don't fit identically. The same is true for kids' clothing. Keep the following tips in mind when you're shopping for them.

- Treat size 6X as the halfway point between size 6 and size 7. Keep in mind that the original intent of 6X was to accommodate the "fuller" child. Some manufacturers still adhere to this practice. Check waistbands for extra girth.
- Be wary of "junior" size looks from filtered-down women's styles. These looks are often too sophisticated and out of proportion for the average child. Kids should look like kids; stick to fuller-fashioned looks in dresses and coats, athletic wear, dirndl and kilt skirtings, suspenders on jeans and skirts, baby doll legging silhouettes, apron/pinafore stylings, and European layered looks. For 10-year-old girls resistant to being "babyfied," try fit 'n' flare dresses or slip dresses over T-shirts that can be layered with vests, cropped cardigans, or twin sweater sets. Palazzo pants are often a favorite with little girls who have advanced tastes. Top them off with blazers, bolero jackets, or cropped tops (no skin showing, please) for a right-off-the-runway look.
- You've probably figured out by now that there's no standardization of sizing in children's clothing. This point is really important when you're buying tights. No matter what the guide on the back of the package tells you is the right size for your child, based on height and weight, it never seems to work out. The only solution is to remove the product from the package (ask the salesperson if you can do this or if he or she would do so) and measure for yourself against the child.

There's nothing worse than pulling those tights out at the last minute before an important event only to find that the crotch doesn't make it past your kid's kneecaps.

- There's a fine line between cool-looking grunge, stylish utilitarian looks, and unkempt bag lady. Learn the difference. (My mom used to call this the Poor Pitiful Pearl Look. Does anyone know who this Pearl lady was?)

Harried over Hairwear? How to Keep Headbands from Slip Slidin' Away

- Determine your child's hair type. A narrow, ill-fitting, flimsy headband will not grab fine hair. The band will fall forward, push ears out, and look sloppy.
- Soft headbands are best for thin, fine hair, provided that the sizing is correct and the lycra content is sufficient enough for head huggability.
- Some headbands are too thick and sit up too high on the head, looking like a modified crown. If there are royal bloodlines in your family, fine. If not, opt for the flattering, tailored-looking headband.
- If the headband has teeth, make sure your child can tolerate them. You may want to allow her to wear it around the store while you shop, just to make sure. (This goes for all headbands. Some kids find that certain headbands give them headaches after a while.)
- Keep your little girls looking neat and hip all summer long with braids. From a solo braid down the back to multiple plaits all over the head, braids are the ideal solution for camp; kids don't have to worry about combing out those impossible knots after swimming. In the evening, unfurl dried braids for a fashionable crimped look.

The Right Steps to Buying the Best Shoes for Kids

There are many myths surrounding the proper care and fit of children's shoes and sneakers. Tom Brunick, director of The Athlete's Foot WearTest Center, answers the most common questions parents have about buying shoes for their children:

Q: Should parents buy a child's shoes at least one size larger to accommodate growth?

A: Parents should buy a child's shoe to fit his or her foot at the time of purchase. When the shoes are too big, the child could trip or suffer ankle rollover. A shoe fits when there's a thumbnail's (the child's thumbnail, not an adult's) length between the longest toe and the end of the toe box on the longest foot.

Q: Does it matter what time of day you buy a child's shoes?

A: Time of day doesn't matter; however, a child should be active for two to three hours before you buy the shoes. The child's foot swells from activity so you get a more accurate fit.

Q: Are more expensive athletic shoes better for a child?

A: The most expensive shoes, even though they have the latest in materials and design, are not necessarily designed to last longer or provide better cushioning and support for a child's foot. A consumer is often paying for cosmetics like flashy design and celebrity endorsements. A mid-priced branded athletic shoe may provide the best fit for the child.

Q: Does a parent need to have a child's foot measured once a year?

A: A child's foot can change size up to 34 times before the age of 10. Children's feet should be measured at least four times a year, even if you don't buy shoes that often.

Here are some more pointers on shoes:

- If slippery-soled party shoes are a problem, you have two options. Buy those sure-grip adhesives (most children's shoe stores carry them for about $2) that you can peel and stick to the bottom portion of the shoe. Or take some sandpaper and rub on the sole until the surface becomes somewhat rough. I prefer the latter method because I have found that over time, the adhesives have a tendency to peel off, and kids may trip on them. If you prefer the adhesives, you may want to try adding a little glue to the adhesive strip for extra adherence.
- When shoe-shopping, a good rule of thumb (or should that be toe?) is if the kid loves them right away, buy them. If your child hesitates, leave the shoes in the store; they may never be worn.
- On a serious note, make a quick shoelace check before embarking on escalators. A stray lace can get caught in the step and you may end up in a hospital emergency room. Remind your kids to tie their laces.

“”

Look Who's Talking Style . . . to Smart Shoppers

Adrienne Berg Weinfeld, Fashion Director of The Larkin Group (producers of the International Kid Fashion Show and International Boutique Show)

One of the most innovative children's stylists who I've long admired is Adrienne Berg Weinfeld. There's no mistaking a magazine model who's been treated to Adrienne's distinctive touch. Adrienne knows how to make kids—all kids—look great without following the same, dull trends. Ms. Weinfeld treated the Smart Shopper to some terrific tips:

- *Accessories rule.* Selecting a great outfit is only half the story. To create a fashion statement as well as an individual one, you need to think carefully about hosiery, shoes, scarves, hats, jewelry, and hairwear.

- Pierced earrings belong on children who are responsible enough to take care of their ears if an infection develops. You rarely see a baby or young child in an upscale fashion ad with earrings on. Earrings are the first thing fashion editors and many photo stylists remove before a photo shoot.

- *Bow Out.* Don't limit yourself to using bows in your daughter's hair. Ms. Weinfeld prefers to take advantage of the latest innovations in hair decorating such as rhinestone clips, Goody's old stand-by tortoise hair clips (great for keeping bangs that are growing out away from the face and neat-looking), plaid and patent clips, satin-covered headbands (skinny or fat), marshmallow headbands, and scarves to wrap around ponytails or to be used as headbands.

- *Think texture.* Forget those thin, nylon and lacy tights. Texture is the way to go for a high-styled look. Thick tights or socks in black, under a nubby jumper paired with clunky, lug-sole shoes or suede desert boots look great with big puffs of pink, blue, or yellow down jackets. (Jeans work well with this look, too.) Finish off with a great pair of sunglasses and lots of braids, and you have a unique, yet fashion-forward, look.

- If you find your child dressing in subdued colors such as navy, brown, or black, you might suggest adding a little color via scarves or brighter tights. You'd be amazed at what a pair of acid green tights can do for a drab-colored jumper or skirt.

- Check out antique and thrift shops for vintage hats to perk up an outfit while giving your child a sense of individuality. (Don't overlook scarves for hair or neck wrapping.)

- Dime stores such as Woolworths' are a fashion-conscious bargain-shopper's paradise when it comes to footwear. Ms. Weinfeld especially likes the vintage-looking sandals and grandma-type shoes. They're cheap and they're funky.

- Parents will be delighted to know that tattoos and body piercing are on the way out! What's on the way in? Jewelry is making a comeback. You can expect to start seeing big bracelets and lots of them.

“”

“”

Look Who's Talking Style . . . to Smart Shoppers

Linda Cass, children's grooming/fashion stylist whose clients include Ford Models (children's division), Gottex, etc.

I watched Ms. Cass in action at a photo shoot and picked up some new tips for grooming and styling kids. Linda explains that all kids need a good haircut, clean hair, an eyebrow brush (maybe a bit of gel to keep brows neat and in place), and a bit of colored lip gloss (for older girls and/or special occasions). As I've already mentioned, curling irons come in handy to add a soft, finishing curl to a young girl's hairstyle. However, they can be damaging to children's fragile hair. Fortunately, there's a safer way to curl your kids' hair: Use the hot-air curling iron and hot-air styling brush by Conair. Hot air is blown through the curl (much like a blow dryer) to create impressive curls, with less chance you'll burn the hair. (Call 800 3-CONAIR for a distributor near you. Prices range from $22–$36 on various models of the hot-air curling iron and brush.) Follow package instructions carefully.

“”

“”

Look Who's Talking Style . . . to Smart Shoppers

Lydia Snyder, make-up artist for celebrities, supermodels, and major women's fashion magazines and catalogs.

Lydia has worked with some of the most beautiful and famous women in the world including Audrey Hepburn, Madonna, and Demi Moore. Watching Ms. Snyder's work, whether it's on tropical beaches or in photographers' studios, one notices that more goes on than simply applying eye shadow and foundation. Ms. Snyder is a true artist whose intent is to enhance everyone's individual beauty. Having been a fan of Ms. Snyder's work through the years, I asked her to contribute some thoughts on the matter of grooming and styling kids. (By the way, Ms. Snyder gets plenty of practice on her own two children, Sofie and Ian.) Here are her pointers:

- Most children look best when their hair is styled after washing. To bring out the best in a good haircut, get kids comfortable with blow dryers at an early age. Avoid using the hottest setting, which can singe hair and burn a child's delicate skin. Try the middle settings for actual drying and the cooler setting at the end to lock the hair in shape. If your child has trouble tolerating the dryer, let the hair dry naturally until almost dry (3/4 dry), then use the blower just at the end to smooth and shape ends. You may need to dry bangs a little sooner than the rest of the head. Just remember to use cooler settings on the bangs, or your child may never allow you to come near with a blow dryer again.
- When it comes to teaching your kids about fashion, try compromising. Let them wear their favorite sports logo, team shirts, or athletic jersey, but pair these items with more fashionable trousers rather than the de rigeur jeans. Or reverse this order and let the kids wear the jeans topped off with a silk shirt. Many kids like this idea because of the opulent and silky soft feel of the silk fabric.

“”

“”

Look Who's Talking Style . . . to Smart Shoppers

Betty Miller, wardrobe supervisor and designer at Nickelodeon Studios

Ms. Miller has worked on the shows Clarissa Explains It All; The Mystery Files of Shelby Woo *(pilot)*, Allegra's Window, Welcome Freshman, Keenan & Carol, *and* You To You.

By now you should be familiar with the Smart Shopper's *credo: It's not a bargain if it doesn't fit and flatter, and of course, it's gotta have style! Who knows more about the latest and up-and-coming styles than the wardrobe stylists at Nickelodeon Studios, where young actors and actresses consistently showcase cutting-edge, innovative designs. How many young girls tune in to watch Melissa Joan Hart as Clarissa for the unique fashion statements alone? This modern-day Gidget shows American teen audiences that it's still possible to look beautiful and express individuality without skin-scarring tattoos and plunging necklines.*

Ms. Miller offers these tips to create the looks made popular on the Nick show, and to turn your real-life kids into smart-looking and fashionable winners. According to Ms. Miller, the password seems to be "cherry pick!" Many looks on the Nick shows are the result of comprehensive shopping trips where the staff picks up great items at a variety of places including malls, specialty shops, vintage and thrift outlets, off-price merchants, chain stores, and any "off-the-wall place." Often times Ms. Miller will find a fabulous garment and build an entire outfit around it. For example, you could go to Old Navy (the lower-priced division of The Gap) for a pair of overalls, then find a funky T-shirt or oversized blouse in a specialty shop, discount store, or sample sale. Then pair those up with a retro jacket from a vintage shop or flea market. In your travels, always keep your eyes open for unusual and fashionable apparel and accessories such as suspenders, hats, vests, and scarves that can add individuality to your child's wardrobe. Even if your kids insist on dressing like their peers, you can encourage them to incorporate some unique item into the uniform-of-the-day for self-expression. Some last tips from Betty:

- Don't be afraid to let girls shop in the boy's or men's department. Fifties retro shirting with bright prints and graphics can look great on girls in combination with pants, shorts, overalls, skirts, and jumpers.

- Most importantly, don't tell kids exactly what to wear. Let them use their own freedom of imagination.

“”

""

Look Who's Talking Style . . . to Smart Shoppers
Gay Empson, Fashion Editor of Child magazine

After nine years of fashion editing and coordinating photo shoots for Child *magazine editorials and covers, Ms. Empson has some very definite opinions about what works and doesn't work for most kids. Here's what she tells* The Smart Shopper:

- Comfort is paramount when it comes to dressing children. Buying bigger, especially for boys who don't like to tuck anything in, is great for style and comfort. For girls, consider matching leggings under dresses and jumpers to take the worry out of playground outings and normal, rambunctious kid play where dresses go flying in the air.
- When shopping with kids, make the experience less stressful by making sure small tummies have been satisfied. Hungry, cranky kids make for a sure-fire shopping disaster. After you feed the kids, let them participate in the shopping expedition by picking out something they like—this keeps them occupied and interested in the selection process. Let kids choose something innocuous such as a hat, hairbow, belt, suspenders, vest, etc.
- Don't push kids ahead by dressing them like miniature adults. Allow the child's personality to come through.
- Certain colors may be difficult for some children to wear. Be watchful of colors like olive green, orange, and black, which has a tendency to drain color from a child's face. Most kids look good in pastels, red, and burgundy.

""

Out Darn Spot!

Did you know that there's a fabric stain hotline for you to call with all your nasty stain problems? The Grundy Lab at the Philadelphia College of Textiles and Science (215-951-2757; Mon.–Fri. 9–4) can answer all your dirty little questions. Another great clean-up trick: Sprinkle talcum powder and cornstarch on a stain immediately to absorb it before it sets. If the stain has already set, try lemon juice, white vinegar or hydrogen peroxide (especially effective on blood), which removes the color from the stain. Don't try this technique on fabrics made of acetate.

CHAPTER SEVEN

PAYING FOR CAMP SHOULDN'T HAVE PARENTS SINGIN' THE SUMMERTIME BLUES

It's never too soon to start making camp plans for the summer, especially if you're interested in getting a price break on tuition and fees. If you assumed financial aid was available only to inner-city families on public assistance, think again. It's time to "de-bunk" this myth and tell you about the availability of financial assistance for middle-income and upper-middle-income working families. Aid is available through scholarships, financial aid, camper-ships and tuition discounts. Many upscale, privately owned day and resident summer camps do offer partial and full tuition assistance based upon need, although the camps don't advertise these programs.

"If you don't ask about scholarship opportunities, you won't get any," says Laurie Edelman, Executive Director of the American Camping Association—NY section. So how do you find out which camps offer financial assistance? Contact the American Camping Association (800 777-CAMP in New York, 508 647-2267 in New England), which offers a free guidance counselor service. The Association can help you select the best camp for your child. It will refer you to camps priced within your budget or to those camps that offer financial assistance.

The ACA also publishes an indispensable directory for camp-hunting parents, called "The Guide to Accredited Camps," which includes a nation-wide list of accredited day and sleep-over camps, trip and travel programs, special-needs programs and special-emphasis camps, along with thumbnail activities and setting descriptions, price ranges, session information, financial aid opportunities and/or scholarship availability. (To order the book, call the ACA Bookstore at 800 428-2267. The book costs $16.95; the bookstore accepts Visa, MasterCard and Discover. The 1997/1998 edition will be available in January 1997.) Some local libraries may also have copies of this guide.

By calling the main ACA office in Martinsville, Indiana (317 342-8456, ext. 330), you can request the phone number of one of the 31 regional offices in the country. Your local ACA office may publish a free booklet describing camps located in your region and may also provide a free guidance and referral service.

If you're looking for camp discounts, it is essential that you begin your search early, no later than January or February of the year your child will attend camp. If you wait until spring, most of the scholarship funds have been distributed.

Once you've selected a camp, be prepared to fill out a questionnaire and, in many cases, submit a recent tax return. The camp will review your request and then offer you an aid package based on your individual needs.

There's absolutely no reason for parents to feel self-conscious about asking for financial help. Almost every activity is far too expensive today, even for two-income families. With the cost of everything skyrocketing, the family budgeter must be an accomplished financial juggler. There's no reason to deprive your child of a wonderful summer experience. The scholarship money is sitting there—available to those smart shoppers savvy enough to ask for it. If you're concerned that your child will be treated differently by counselors, or even teased by other campers, forget it! Unless you broadcast the fact that your child was awarded financial aid, no one, except the owner/director or financial aid director, will ever know.

You should also be aware of C.I.T. (counselor in training) tuition discounts. For children as young as age 13 up through age 18, many camps will offer a significant price break on camp fees for those children participating in C.I.T. programs. Usually, camps offer this opportunity to campers who have attended the camp for several seasons and are familiar with the camp and the routine. However, camps will consider accepting mature and competent new campers into C.I.T. programs. If your child falls into this age range, be sure to inquire. You could save up to 70% off camp tuition!

Additional Resources

Peterson's Summer Opportunities for Kids and Teenagers (Phone 800-338-3282; $24.95) is a good resource to have handy. This guidebook features over 1,600 Summer programs, complete with detailed financial aid information for individual camps.

Peterson's Education Center also has a Summer programs section at its Web site (http://www.petersons.com).

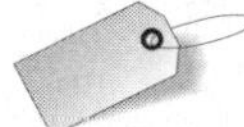

Bargain Byte

There is a perfect camp for every child. For example, if your kid is nervous about going away for the summer, consider a sleep-over camp that lets your child come home for weekends. Campus Kids, in South Kent, CT (phone number (800) 633-7350 Sept.–June; (860) 927-5331 or (908) 850-5872 July–Aug.; Internet campuskids@aol.com), is one such camp. Remember, your key focus should be finding the best camp for your child's specific interests. After you narrow down your choices, ask about the fees. Even if the camp is way out of your financial league, the camp may give you some form of financial aid to accommodate your child. Many camps don't announce financial aid opportunities in the camp guide books even though they have them. So don't forget to ask!

Big Top Bargain

Ladies and gentlemen, and children of all ages! Step right up and claim your child's free circus ticket! Did you know that every baby born in 1996, 1997 and probably 1998 is entitled to receive his or her first ticket to the Ringling Bros. and Barnum & Bailey circus absolutely free? The free admission offer is redeemable at any time during the child's lifetime—whether they claim it at ages 2 or 92! Parents need to mail their name, address, newborn's name and date of birth to:

Ringling Bros. and Barnum & Bailey
P.O. Box 39845
Edina, MN 55439-9458

Parents will get a certificate exchangeable for one ticket to any performance in any city in any year. Leave it to the greatest show on Earth to come up with the greatest deal on Earth!

Share Your Finds!

If you'd like to contact the *Smart Shopper's Guide* with your favorite bits of bargain information in any category, we'd love to hear from you! Indeed we'd be happy to make your discovery a part of the next edition of this book. Contact us at: P.O. Box 797 Forest Hills, NY 11375.

Get Kid News All Year Long

To subscribe to my bi-monthly newsletter "Kid News—A Children's Bargain Guide," which will keep you posted on the latest sale events and bargains throughout the country including exact dates, times, addresses, phone numbers and specific merchandise description, send a check for $26.95 for a one-year subscription to:

KID NEWS
P.O. Box 797
Forest Hills, NY 11375

Editors are on tap all year long for personal assistance. If you see something you love at a retailer and want to find it for less, we'll direct you to a convenient source.

INDEX

NOTES

INDEX

NOTES

NOTES

NOTES